FOR MY PARENTS

Published in 2008 by Stewart, Tabori & Chang
An imprint of Harry N. Abrams, Inc.

Library of Congress Cataloging-in-Publication Data:

Melanson, Robin.
  Knitting new mittens and gloves : warm and adorn your
  hands in 28 innovative ways / Robin Melanson.
      p. cm.
  Includes bibliographical references.
  ISBN 978-1-58479-666-4 (alk. paper)
  1. Knitting--Patterns. 2. Mittens. 3. Gloves. I. Title.
  TT825.M413 2008
  746.43'2041--dc22

  2007019273

Editors: Melanie Falick and Liana Allday
Designer: Sarah Von Dreele
Production Manager: Jacquie Poirier

The text of this book was composed in Futura
and Janson.

Printed and bound in China

10 9 8 7 6 5 4 3 2 1

HNA
harry n. abrams, inc.
a subsidiary of La Martinière Groupe
115 West 18th Street
New York, NY 10011
www.hnabooks.com

KNITTING NEW
MITTENS & GLOVES

WARM AND ADORN YOUR HANDS IN 28 INNOVATIVE WAYS

ROBIN MELANSON

PHOTOGRAPHS BY TYLLIE BARBOSA

PHOTO-STYLING BY KELLY McKAIG

STC Craft/A Melanie Falick Book | Stewart, Tabori & Chang | New York

TABLE OF CONTENTS

6 INTRODUCTION

9 ACCOMPLICE
13 AETHELWYNE
17 ÅLESUND
21 ALTERNATING CURRENT
25 BLACKTHORN
29 BOX PLEATS
35 BRÜNNHILDE
41 CEANGALTAS
45 CHEVALIER
49 DRIVER
55 EVENING LIGHT
61 FILIGREE
65 GLAISTIG
69 GOLDEN BRACELETS
73 GOTHIC
77 GRETEL
81 HOUNDSTOOTH MISCELLANY
85 JACK-IN-THE-BOX
91 NEGATIVE SPACE
95 PLUSH
99 POPPY
103 RUSALKA
107 SHELTIE
111 SNUG
115 STANDARD DEVIATION
119 STRATA
125 TAPISSERIE
129 WELIG

134 SELECTING MATERIALS
135 SPECIAL TECHNIQUES
141 ABBREVIATIONS
142 INDEX OF PROJECTS BY YARN WEIGHT
143 SOURCES FOR SUPPLIES
144 BIBLIOGRAPHY
144 ACKNOWLDEGMENTS

INTRODUCTION

When the possibility of writing a book of new mitten and glove patterns was presented to me, I was immediately intrigued as I consider myself a mitten and glove aficionado of sorts. I grew up in Cape Breton, on Canada's Atlantic coast, where winters tend to be harsh and mittens and gloves are essential in everyone's wardrobes. I recognized right away that this would be a wonderful opportunity for me to explore new avenues of design and to share my enthusiasm for these humble items.

Like many knitters, I am especially drawn to mittens and gloves because they are useful, generally quick to make, small enough to carry around while being worked on and to work on even in warm weather without discomfort, and don't require a lot of yarn. They are also a great project on which to experiment—to try out new techniques or yarns that can be applied later to larger endeavors. Since I prefer not to knit the same project over and over again, I'm always stimulated by a fresh challenge and by the opportunity to view something familiar with a new perspective. When I accepted the opportunity to work on this book, I set the following goal: to redefine how mittens and gloves are made and worn by experimenting with and mixing and matching traditional and nontraditional techniques and influences. On the pages that follow are the results. For example, on page 91 is Negative Space, a design inspired by a unique but rarely seen Norwegian folk mitten with a cutaway palm. On page 115 is Standard Deviation, influenced by a combination of the hotel carpeting in the horror movie *The Shining* and my love of stranded colorwork and Norwegian wool. For Gothic on page 73, I challenged the utilitarian boundary of the glove: This design is intended as a purely decorative accessory rather than a winter essential.

As you may have already guessed by scanning the project list on page 4 or the photos or descriptive passages throughout the book, I have a passion for Celtic language and art that always seems to make its way to the surface, whether it is the direct inspiration for a design—like Golden Bracelets (page 69) or Ceangaltas (page 41)—or an influence in my choice of colors, buttons, or project names. I have also spent a lot of time reading medieval European literature, Norse and Icelandic sagas, and Early Irish heroic cycles. Often I am inspired by a name, a character, or an interesting description, or even just by thinking about a particular era in history. I follow fashion with interest but not slavishly; I pay the most attention to avant-garde runway shows with models sprouting antlers or donning designs incorporating futuristic shapes with intricate hand-finished details. While these interests do not always translate directly into my knitting, they do inform my outlook on design and my general aesthetic.

As I began the adventure of designing the projects for this book, I recalled reading in the science-fiction novel *The Terminal Experiment* by Robert. J. Sawyer that the funniest jokes are created when an unexpected association causes the brain to generate a new pathway, which translates as humor. I think the same is true when creating new knitwear designs: An inventive combination of familiar styles and materials produces a sense of freshness and originality that may not have been evident within any of the components individually. I think you will find that the designs that follow are fresh but not faddish, unusual but not outlandish. They are grounded in history and technique, but each has some new element or combination wrought into it. I hope that working on these mittens and gloves will inspire in you an ever-increasing fondness for and fascination with them. That is certainly how designing and knitting them has rewarded me.

ACCOMPLICE

These easy-to-make hand-warmers can be worn
with or without gloves underneath. Worked in
a luscious silk/mohair blend yarn, they keep the
wrist and forearm warm and sweep gracefully
over the top of the hand. The barred pattern is
created by passing yarnovers over the subsequent
stitches, making a channel of yarn floats. The
hand edge is finished with a few rows of a slipped
stitch pattern, and the thumb hole is created
by making a few chain stitches from the last stitch
of the bind-off row and attaching it to a spot on
the opposite side.

thumbhole
bar stitch
linen stitch

SIZES
One size (to fit average woman)

FINISHED MEASUREMENTS
Approximately 7¾" wrist circumference; approximately 9¼" hand circumference

YARN
Fleece Artist Kid Silk 3-ply (70% kid mohair / 30% silk; 220 yards [201 meters] / 100 grams): 1 hank vintage

NEEDLES
One set of four double-pointed needles (dpn) size US 7 (4.5 mm)
Change needle size if necessary to obtain correct gauge.

NOTIONS
Crochet hook size US 7 (4.5 mm); stitch marker

GAUGE
18 sts and 24 rnds = 4" (10 cm) in Barred Pattern

STITCH PATTERNS

Barred Pattern
(multiple of 5 sts; 2-rnd repeat)
Rnd 1: Knit.
Rnd 2: *Yo, k2, pass yo over last 2 sts worked, k3; repeat from * around.
Repeat Rnds 1 and 2 for Barred Pattern.

Linen Stitch
(multiple of 2 sts; 2-rnd repeat)
Rnd 1: *K1, slip 1 purlwise wyif; repeat from * around.
Rnd 2: *Slip 1 purlwise wyif, k1; repeat from * around.
Repeat Rnds 1 and 2 for Linen Stitch.

HAND WARMERS (BOTH ALIKE)
With Long-Tail CO (see page 136), CO 35 sts, divide among 3 needles [12-12-11]. Join for working in the rnd, being careful not to twist sts; place marker (pm) for beginning of rnd. Begin Barred Pattern. Work even for 31 rows (work should measure approximately 5¼" from the beginning).
Increase Rnd: *Yo, k2, pass yo over last 2 sts worked, k2, M1L, k1; repeat from * around–42 sts.
Next Rnd: Knit.
Next Rnd: *Yo, k2, pass yo over last 2 sts worked, k4; repeat from * around.
Repeat last 2 rnds 6 times. Knit 1 rnd.
Next Rnd: Change to Linen st. Work even for 5 rnds.
BO 41 sts–1 st remains. Cut yarn, leaving a long tail. Insert crochet hook into last st and ch 6. Fasten off. Sew end of chain approximately 12 sts away from beginning of chain along BO edge, creating a thumb hole.

Aethelwyne

An elfin shape and a rustic yarn combine
to create an otherworldly mitten, which will
nonetheless keep both children and adults
warm in this realm. The bobble ring crowning
the fluted cuff represents a fairy ring, which
is a ring of mushrooms, in the center of which
no mushrooms grow and fairies are said
to dance. Aethelwyne is an Old English name
meaning "friend of the elves."

∧∧∧∧∧∧∧∧∧∧∧

SIZES

Small (Medium, Large)
To fit Small Child (Medium Child, Woman)

FINISHED MEASUREMENTS

Approximately 5½ (6½, 7½)"
circumference

YARN

Harrisville Designs New England Highland
(100% wool; 200 yards [183 meters] /
100 grams): 1 hank #07 tundra
(#74 rose, #15 loden blue)

NEEDLES

One set of five double-pointed needles
(dpn) size US 6 (4 mm)
One set of five double-pointed needles
size US 5 (3.75 mm)
Change needle size if necessary to obtain
correct gauge.

NOTIONS

Stitch marker; waste yarn in
contrasting color

GAUGE

20 sts and 28 rnds = 4" (10 cm) in
Stockinette stitch (St st) using larger needles

ABBREVIATIONS

(MB) Make Bobble: [K1, p1, k1] in
next st, turn work, k3, turn work, p3,
pass first and second sts over third st
and off the needle.

All sts are slipped purlwise with yarn in
back unless otherwise indicated.

Right Mitten

CUFF

With smaller needles and Long-Tail CO (see page 136),
CO 30 (35, 45) sts, divide among 3 needles [10-10-10
(15-10-10, 15-15-15)]. Join for working in the rnd,
being careful not to twist sts; place marker (pm) for
beginning of rnd.

Begin Pattern: *K3, p2; repeat from * around.
Work even for 12 (13, 15) rnds.
Decrease Rnd: *K3, p2tog; repeat from * around–
24 (28, 36) sts.
Next Rnd: *K3, p1; repeat from * around.
Work even for 1 (2, 3) rnds.
Bobble Rnd: *K1, MB, k1, p1; repeat from * around.
Next Rnd: *K1, slip 1, k1, p1; repeat from * around.
Next Rnd: *K3, p1; repeat from * around.
Work even for 0 (1, 2) rnds.

HAND

Increase Rnd: Change to larger needles and St st
(knit every rnd). *K1 (1, 0), M1R, k10 (12, 18), M1L,
k1 (1, 18); repeat from * 1 (1, 0) time–28 (32, 38) sts.
Redistribute sts among 4 needles [7-7-7-7 (8-8-8-8,
10-9-10-9)]. Work even until piece measures approximately 1¼ (1½, 2½)" from end of Cuff.

THUMB OPENING

Next Rnd: K15 (17, 20), change to waste yarn and
k5 (6, 7), slip these 5 (6, 7) sts back to left-hand needle,
change to working yarn, knit these 5 (6, 7) sts again,
knit to end. Work even until piece measures approximately 2¾ (3¼, 5)" from end of Cuff.

MITTEN TOP

Next Rnd: *K5 (14, 17), k2tog; repeat from *
around–24 (30, 36) sts remain. Work even for 1 rnd.
Next Rnd: *K4, k2tog, repeat from * around–20
(25, 30) sts remain. Work even for 3 rnds.
Next Rnd: *K3, k2tog; repeat from * around–16
(20, 24) sts remain. Work even for 3 rnds.

Next Rnd: *K2, K2tog; repeat from * around–12 (15, 18) sts remain. Work even for 3 rnds.
Next Rnd: *K1, k2tog; repeat from * around–8 (10, 12) sts remain. Work even for 3 rnds.
Next Rnd: *K2tog; repeat from * around–4 (5, 6) sts remain. Cut yarn, leaving a 6" tail. Draw through remaining sts, pull tight and fasten off.

Thumb
Carefully remove waste yarn from Thumb sts and place bottom 5 (6, 7) sts and top 6 (7, 8) sts onto 2 larger dpns, being careful not to twist sts. Rejoin yarn to bottom sts, pick up and knit 1 (1, 2) sts at side of Thumb Opening, knit across 5 (6, 7) bottom sts, pick up and knit 1 (1, 2) sts at other side of Thumb Opening, knit across 6 (7, 8) top sts–13 (15, 19) sts. Redistribute sts evenly among 3 dpns. Join for working in the rnd; pm for beginning of rnd.

Children's Sizes Only
Decrease Rnd 1: K2tog, k3 (4), ssk, k6 (7)–11 (13) sts remain. Work even in St st until piece is long enough to cover thumb.
Decrease Rnd 2: *K2tog; repeat from * to last st, k1–6 (7) sts remain. Cut yarn, leaving a 6" tail. Draw through remaining sts, pull tight, fasten off.

Woman's Size Only
Decrease Rnd 1: K1, k2tog, k5, ssk, k2tog, k6, ssk (last st of this rnd together with first st of next rnd)–15 sts remain. Work even in St st until piece is ¼" from end of thumb (approximately 14 more rnds).
Decrease Rnd 2: *K1, k2tog; repeat from * around–10 sts remain. Work even for 3 rnds.
Decrease Rnd 3: *K2tog; repeat from * around–5 sts remain. Cut yarn, leaving a 6" tail. Draw through remaining sts, pull tight and fasten off.

Left Mitten
Work as for Right Mitten to Thumb Opening.

Thumb Opening
Next Rnd: K22 (25, 30), change to waste yarn, k5 (6, 7), slip these 5 (6, 7) sts back to left-hand needle, change to working yarn, knit these 5 (6, 7) sts again, knit to end. Complete as for Right Mitten.

Finishing
Weave in ends. Block mittens.

Ålesund

These multicolored mittens have traditional Norwegian roots. The Art Nouveau-style motif on the top of the hand—definitely a modern touch—is an unexpected counterpoint to the striped palm. The cuff is edged with a few rows of gently flaring Stockinette stitch, which in this robust yarn is easy to block flat. The main pattern is knitted in two colors, and additional colors are added later using duplicate stitch. The mitten is named for a Norwegian town that was (and is today) an important center in the *Jugendstil* ("youth style") movement, a German variant of Art Nouveau.

One size (to fit average woman)

FINISHED MEASUREMENTS
Approximately 7¾" circumference

YARN
Rauma 3-ply Strikkegarn (100% wool; 115 yards [105 meters] / 50 grams): 2 balls #136 black (MC); 1 ball each #140 mauve (A), #180 wine (B), #146 gold (C), and #150 acid yellow (D)

NEEDLES
One set of five double-pointed needles (dpn) size US 3 (3.25 mm)
One set of five double-pointed needles size US 4 (3.5 mm)
One set of five double-pointed needles size US 6 (4 mm)
Change needle size if necessary to obtain correct gauge.

NOTIONS
Stitch markers; waste yarn in contrasting color

GAUGE
24 sts and 25 rnds = 4" (10 cm) in Stockinette stitch (St st) over Fair Isle Chart using size US 4 (3.5 mm) needles

STITCH PATTERN

Corrugated Rib Pattern
(multiple of 4 sts; 12-rnd repeat)
Rnd 1: *K2 with MC, k2 with A; repeat from * around.
Rnds 2-5: *K2 with MC, p2 with A; repeat from * around.
Rnds 6 and 7: *K2 with MC, p2 with B; repeat from * around. Cut B after Rnd 7.
Rnds 8-12: Repeat Rnd 2.

2-Color Palm Pattern
(multiple of 2 sts + 1; 1-rnd repeat)
All Rnds: K1 with A, *k1 with MC, k1 with A; repeat from * around.

Right Mitten

CUFF
With MC, Long-Tail CO (see page 136), and largest dpns, CO 44 sts, divide among 4 dpns (12-10-12-10). Join for working in the rnd, being careful not to twist sts; place marker (pm) for beginning of rnd. Begin St st; work even for 4 rnds.
Next Rnd: Change to smallest needles and Corrugated Rib Pattern. Work even for 12 rnds.

HAND
Next Rnd: Change to size US 4 (3.5 mm) needles and MC. *K22, M1L; repeat from * around–46 sts.
Next Rnd: Work Fair Isle Chart across 23 sts, pm, change to 2-Color Palm Pattern, work to end.
Next Rnd: Continuing Fair Isle Chart as established, work 23 sts, slip marker (sm), change to 2-Color Palm Pattern, work to end. Work even until Rnd 17 of Chart is complete.

THUMB OPENING
Rnd 18: Work 23 sts, k1 with A, transfer next 9 sts to waste yarn for Thumb, CO 9 sts over gap using Backward Loop CO (see page 136), alternating MC and A, corresponding to color of st being replaced, work to end. Work even until Row 39 of Chart is complete.

SHAPE MITTEN TOP
Decrease Rnd 1: Working decreases as shown in Chart, work to first marker, sm, k1 with A, ssk with MC, work to last 3 sts, k2tog with MC, k1 with A–42 sts remain. Repeat Decrease Rnd 1 every rnd 8 times–10 sts remain.

Decrease Rnd 2: Work to first marker, sm, k1 with A, dcd with MC, k1 with A–6 sts remain. Cut both yarns, leaving long tails. With MC, draw through remaining sts, pull tight and fasten off. Weave in ends on WS.

THUMB

Transfer sts from waste yarn to dpn. Rejoin MC and A. Beginning at side of Thumb with A, pick up and knit 2 sts from gap (not from sts CO above Thumb), knit across Thumb sts in appropriate colors, with A, pick up and knit 2 sts from gap at other side of Thumb, pick up and knit 9 sts from sts CO above Thumb using appropriate colors and picking up from the middle of each stitch–22 sts.

Decrease Rnd 1: Ssk with A, knit next 9 sts in established colors, k2tog with A, knit next 9 sts in established colors–20 sts remain. Work even until piece measures approximately 2½", or until piece is long enough to cover tip of thumb. Cut A, leaving long tail.

Decrease Rnd 2: *With MC, k2tog; repeat from * around–10 sts remain. Cut yarn, leaving long tail. With MC, draw through remaining sts, pull tight and fasten off. Weave in ends on WS.

Left Mitten

Work as for Right Mitten to Thumb Opening.

THUMB OPENING

Next Rnd: Work 23 sts, work in 2-Color Palm Pattern across 13 sts, transfer next 9 sts to waste yarn for Thumb, CO 9 sts over gap using Backward Loop CO, alternating MC and A, corresponding to color of st being replaced, work to end. Complete as for Right Mitten.

FINISHING

Block Mittens to even out sts prior to working Duplicate Stitch (see page 137). Pay special attention to flare at lower edge of Mittens; pin flat and steam with iron (set on wool) and damp cloth. When Mittens are dry, work Duplicate Stitch as indicated in Chart.

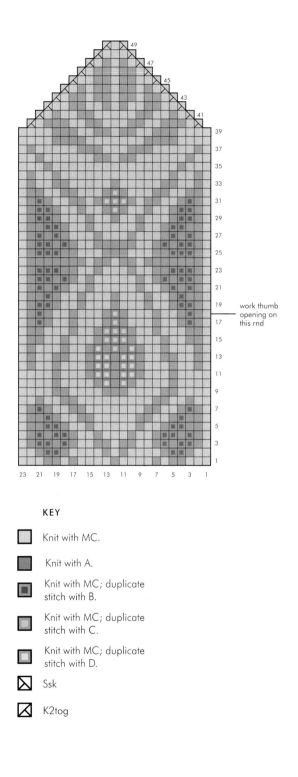

work thumb opening on this rnd

KEY

- ☐ Knit with MC.
- ■ Knit with A.
- ▣ Knit with MC; duplicate stitch with B.
- ▣ Knit with MC; duplicate stitch with C.
- ▫ Knit with MC; duplicate stitch with D.
- ⊠ Ssk
- ⊠ K2tog

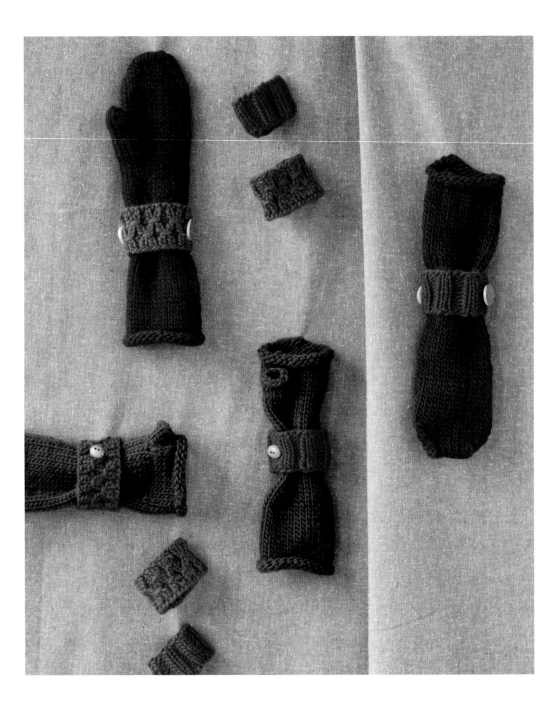

ALTERNATING CURRENT

Two different mittens are presented here:
a full mitten and a fingerless mitten. Buttons
at the wrist allow the cuffs to be changed
like bracelets. Make both types of cuffs
in different colors, then alternate them to suit
your mood. The fingerless version could be
worn indoors in a chilly workplace or outside
when you need your fingers free.

smocking

SIZES
One size (to fit average woman)

FINISHED MEASUREMENTS
Approximately 8" circumference

YARN
Brown Sheep Company Lamb's Pride Bulky (85% wool / 15% mohair; 125 yards [114 meters] / 113 grams): Mittens: 2 skeins #M-185 aubergine (MC), 1 skein #M-175 bronze patina (A); Fingerless Mittens: 2 skeins #M-58 ink blue (MC), 1 skein #M-25 garnet (A); Cuffs also shown in #M-23 fuchsia (A)

NEEDLES
One set of five double-pointed needles (dpn) size US 10½ (6.5 mm) Change needle size if necessary to obtain correct gauge.

NOTIONS
Stitch marker; waste yarn; cable needle (cn); four ¾" buttons

GAUGE
13 sts and 19 rnds = 4" (10 cm) in Stockinette stitch (St st)

Full Mittens

LEFT MITTEN
With MC and Long-Tail CO (see page 136), CO 26 sts, divide among 4 needles [7-6-7-6]. Join for working in the rnd, being careful not to twist sts; place marker (pm) for beginning of rnd. *[Note: Needles 1 and 2 form the back of the Mitten; Needles 3 and 4 form the palm.]*

Begin St st (knit every rnd). Work even until piece measures approximately 9" from the beginning, or to desired length to base of thumb.

Thumb Opening
Next Rnd: K21, change to waste yarn and k4, slip these 4 sts back to left-hand needle, change to working yarn, knit these 4 sts again, k1. Work even until piece measures 3½" from Thumb Opening, or until Mitten reaches first knuckle of middle finger.

Mitten Top
Decrease Rnd: Ssk, knit to last 2 sts on Needle 2, k2tog, ssk, knit to last 2 sts on Needle 4, k2tog—22 sts remain. Knit 1 rnd. Repeat Decrease Rnd every other rnd twice—14 sts remain.

Transfer sts from Needle 2 to Needle 1 and sts from Needle 4 to Needle 3. Graft sts together using Kitchener Stitch (see page 139).

Thumb
Carefully remove waste yarn from Thumb sts and place bottom 4 sts and top 5 sts onto 2 dpns, being careful not to twist sts. Rejoin yarn to bottom sts, pick up and knit 1 st at side of Thumb Opening, knit across 4 bottom sts, pick up and knit 1 st at other side of Thumb Opening, knit across 5 top sts—11 sts. Redistribute sts among 3 dpns. Join for working in the rnd; pm for beginning of rnd.

Next Rnd: K2tog, k2, ssk, k5–9 sts remain. Work even until piece is long enough to cover thumb.
Next Rnd: *K2tog; repeat from * to last st, k1–5 sts remain. Cut yarn, leaving a 6" tail. Draw through remaining sts, pull tight and fasten off.

RIGHT MITTEN
Work as for Left Mitten to Thumb Opening. *[Note: Terms for "back of hand" and "palm" should be reversed.]*

Thumb Opening
Next Rnd: K14, change to A and k4, slip these 4 sts back to left-hand needle, change to working yarn, knit these 4 sts again, knit to end. Complete as for Left Mitten.

Fingerless Mittens

LEFT MITTEN
Work as for Left Full Mitten until piece measures 2¼" from Thumb Opening, or until Mitten covers base of fingers. BO all sts.

Thumb
Work as for Full Mitten until 9 sts remain. Work even for 3 rnds. BO all sts.

RIGHT MITTEN
Work as for Right Full Mitten until piece measures 2¼" from Thumb Opening, or until Mitten covers base of fingers. Complete as for Left Fingerless Mitten.

Smocked Cuffs (make 2)

With A, CO 32 sts, divide among 4 needles [8-8-8-8]. Join for working in the rnd, being careful not to twist sts; pm for beginning of rnd.

Rnds 1-3: *K1, p1; repeat from * around.
Rnd 4: *Transfer next 3 sts to cn, wrap yarn once around these sts counterclockwise (pulling gently), transfer these sts to right-hand needle, p1; repeat from * around.
Rnd 5: *K1, p1; repeat from * around.
Rnd 6 (Buttonhole Rnd): *[K1, p1] 7 times, ssk, yo; repeat from * around.
Rnd 7: *K1, p1; repeat from * around.
Rnd 8: Slip first st of rnd to Needle 4, *p1, transfer next 3 sts to cn, wrap yarn once around these sts counterclockwise (pulling gently), transfer these sts to right-hand needle; repeat from * around. *[Note: Sts may need to be redistributed among the needles for wrapping.]* Transfer last st on Needle 4 back to Needle 1.
Rnds 9-10: *K1, p1; repeat from * around. BO all sts in pattern.

Ribbed Cuffs (make 2)

With A, CO 24 sts, divide among 4 needles [6-6-6-6]. Join for working in the rnd, being careful not to twist sts; pm for beginning of rnd.

Rnd 1: *K2, p2; repeat from * around.
Work even for 2 rnds.
Buttonhole Rnd: *[K2, p2] 2 times, k2, yo, p2tog; repeat from * around. Work even for 4 rnds. BO all sts in pattern.

FINISHING
Weave in ends. Sew a button to each side of wrist. Pull Cuff on and button at wrist.

BLACKTHORN

The blackthorn is a tree that produces the small fruit known as sloe berries, from which sloe gin is made. A cocktail of the same name is made from sloe gin and sweet vermouth. These fitted gloves, worked in a lovely and strong Shetland wool with the unusual addition of leather lacing on the back of the hand, remind me of that cocktail: a mysterious elixir with a sharp name, not overly sweet.

batwing edges

SIZES

Women's Small/Medium (Large)

FINISHED MEASUREMENTS

Approximately 7¼ (8)" circumference

YARN

Jamieson's Shetland Double Knitting
(100% pure Shetland wool; 82 yards
[75 meters] / 25 grams): 3 balls #293
port wine (MC)
Jamieson's Shetland Spindrift (100% pure
Shetland wool; 115 yards [105 meters] /
25 grams): 1 ball #238 osprey (A)

NEEDLES

One set of five double-pointed needles
(dpn) size US 4 (3.5 mm)
One pair straight needles size US 1½
(2.5 mm)
Change needle size if necessary to obtain
correct gauge.

NOTIONS

Stitch markers; waste yarn in contrasting
color; crochet hook size US B/1
(2.25 mm), for picking up sts; 1 yard
(1 meter) leather lacing

GAUGE

24 sts and 32 rows = 4" (10 cm) in
Stockinette stitch (St st) using larger
needles and MC
32 sts and 44 rows = 4" (10 cm) in
Stockinette stitch using smaller
needles and A

STITCH PATTERN

1x1 Rib
(multiple of 2 sts; 1-rnd repeat)
All Rnds: *K1, p1; repeat from * around.

Left Glove

With Long-Tail CO (see page 136), dpn, and MC,
CO 44 (48) sts, divide among 4 needles [11-11-11-11
(12-12-12-12)]. Join for working in the rnd, being
careful not to twist sts; place marker (pm) for beginning
of rnd. *[Note: Needles 1 and 2 hold the sts for the palm
and Thumb, and Needles 3 and 4 hold the sts for the
back of the hand.]* Begin 1x1 Rib. Work even for 4 rnds.
Next Rnd: Change to St st; work even for 7 rnds.
Decrease Rnd 1: *K9 (10), k2tog; repeat from *
around–40 (44) sts remain. Work even for 7 rnds.
Decrease Rnd 2: *K8 (9), k2tog; repeat from *
around–36 (40) sts remain. Work even for 7 rnds.
Increase Rnd 1: *K9 (10), M1L; repeat from *
around–40 (44) sts. Work even for 2 rnds.
Increase Rnd 2: K5, *M1L, k10 (11); repeat from *
to last 5 (6) sts, M1L, knit to end–44 (48) sts. Work
even for 2 rnds.

SHAPE THUMB

Increase Rnd 1: K20 (22), pm, M1L, k2, M1R, pm,
knit to end–46 (50) sts. Work even for 2 rnds.
Increase Rnd 2: Knit to first marker, slip marker (sm),
M1L, knit to second marker, M1R, sm, knit to end.
Repeat last 3 rnds 5 times–58 (62) sts. Knit 1 rnd.
Next Rnd: K20 (22), transfer next 16 sts to waste yarn,
CO 2 sts over gap, knit to end–44 (48) sts remain.
Work even until piece is long enough to reach base of
Pinkie, ending 5 (6) sts before end of rnd, removing
all markers on last rnd.

DIVIDE FOR FINGERS

Pinkie: Transfer next 10 (12) sts [last 5 (6) sts of
rnd and first 5 (6) sts of next rnd] to waste yarn, pm,
CO 2 sts over gap, knit to 5 sts before marker.
Ring Finger: Transfer next 12 sts [5 sts from back,
2 CO sts from previous rnd, and 5 sts from palm] to
waste yarn, removing marker, pm, CO 2 sts over gap,
knit to 5 (6) sts before marker.

Middle Finger: Transfer next 12 (14) sts [5 (6) sts from back, 2 CO sts from previous rnd, and 5 (6) sts from palm] to waste yarn, pm, CO 2 sts over gap–16 sts remain for Index Finger.

INDEX FINGER

Work in St st until piece is long enough to cover index finger (approximately 22 rnds).

Decrease Rnd: *K2tog; repeat from * to end–8 sts remain. Cut yarn, leaving a 6" tail. Draw through remaining sts, pull tight and fasten off, with tail to the inside.

MIDDLE, RING, AND PINKIE FINGERS, AND THUMB

Working one finger at a time, transfer sts from waste yarn to dpns. Rejoin MC; pick up and knit 2 sts from CO between previous Finger and current Finger (or from sts CO over gap for Thumb)–14 (16) sts for Middle Finger [14 sts for Ring Finger; 12 (14) sts for Pinkie; 18 sts for Thumb]. Join for working in the rnd; pm for beginning of rnd. Work in St st until piece is long enough to cover finger (approximately 27 rnds for Middle Finger, 25 rnds for Ring Finger, 21 rnds for Pinkie, and 20 rnds for Thumb). Complete as for Index Finger–7 (8) sts remain for Middle Finger [7 sts for Ring Finger; 6 (7) sts for Pinkie; 9 sts for Thumb].

Right Glove

Work as for Left Glove to beginning of Thumb Shaping.

SHAPE THUMB

Increase Rnd 1: K22 (24), pm, M1L, k2, M1R, pm, knit to end–46 (50) sts. Complete as for Left Glove, working Fingers in the same order. *[Note: Terms for "back of hand" and "palm" should be reversed.]*

FINISHING

Block Gloves.

Lacers

LEFT GLOVE

Thumb Side: With RS facing, using crochet hook and A, beginning where Thumb Opening ends and ending near base of Thumb, pick up 25 sts from between the first and second st columns to the left of the Thumb, as follows: Working with A on RS, insert crochet hook under the horizontal strand between the sts, draw up a loop and leave on hook. Work into every row, working from right to left. Transfer the 25 sts to straight needle, making sure that working yarn is at tip of needle, ready to work a WS row.

Rows 1, 3, and 5 (WS): Purl.
Rows 2 and 4: Knit.
Row 6: K3, *[k1, p1, k1] into next st, k5; repeat from * to last 4 sts, [k1, p1, k1] into next st, k3–33 sts.
Row 7: Purl.
Row 8: K4, *[k1, p1, k1] into next st, k7; repeat from * to last 5 sts, [k1, p1, k1] into next st, k4–41 sts. BO all sts knitwise.

Heel of Hand Side: Pick up 25 sts as for Thumb side, reversing direction of pick-up [beginning even with base of Thumb and ending even with end of Thumb Opening], working between last 2 st columns of back of hand. Complete as for Thumb side.

Repeat for Right Glove, picking up sts for Thumb side from base of Thumb to end of Thumb Opening, and sts for heel of hand side from even with end of Thumb Opening to even with base of Thumb.

Lace leather ties through the holes created under the increases on Row 8, working from knuckles to wrist. Tie at wrist.

BOX PLEATS

A box pleat ornaments the cuff of these fingerless gloves: It is created by knitting together stitches from three layers that have been placed on spare needles and folded into the pleat shape. The back of the hand is decorated with a beaded twisted stitch pattern, and beads are incorporated into the bind-off as well.

One size (to fit average woman)

FINISHED MEASUREMENTS
Approximately 7½" circumference

YARN
Dale of Norway Svale (50% cotton / 40% viscose / 10% silk; 114 yards [104 meters] / 50 grams): 2 balls #2846 copper

NEEDLES
One pair straight needles size US 4 (3.5 mm)
One set of five double-pointed needles (dpn) size US 4 (3.5 mm)
Change needle size if necessary to obtain correct gauge.

NOTIONS
Crochet hook size US E/4 (3.5 mm); stitch markers; cable needle (cn); 120 size 8/0 beads in coordinating color; wire beading needle; needle-nose pliers (for crushing off misshapen beads); waste yarn in contrasting color

GAUGE
23 sts and 30 rnds = 4" (10 cm) in Stockinette stitch (St st)
Beaded Twist Stitch Chart measures approximately 1⅜" wide

PREPARE BEADS
Thread yarn through wire beading needle, then thread half of beads onto yarn. Keep pushing beads down yarn until they are required. Thread other half of beads onto second ball of yarn to use for second Glove, as you will not want to have to restring when you need to start a new ball. For more information, see page 135.

Right Glove

CUFF
With straight needles and Long-Tail CO (see page 136), CO 52 sts. Begin St st, beginning with a WS row and slipping last st of each row purlwise. Work even for 7 rows.

Next Row (RS): K5, transfer next 8 sts onto 2 dpns (4 sts each), fold second dpn forward towards left-hand needle so that RS's are together, and fold first dpn towards second dpn so that WS's are together (you will have 3 layers arranged accordion-style, in the following order: first dpn, second dpn, left-hand needle), then [k3tog (1 st from each needle)] 4 times, place next 8 sts onto 2 dpns [4-4], fold second dpn back towards left-hand needle so that WS's are together, and fold first dpn towards second dpn so that RS's are together (the order is reversed from the first pleat: left-hand needle, second dpn, first dpn), then [k3tog (1 st from each needle)] 4 times, knit to end–36 sts remain.
Next Row: *K1, p1-tbl; repeat from * to last 2 sts, k2.
Next Row: P2, *k1-tbl, p1; repeat from * to end.

Repeat last 2 rows once.

BEADED TWIST STITCH CHART

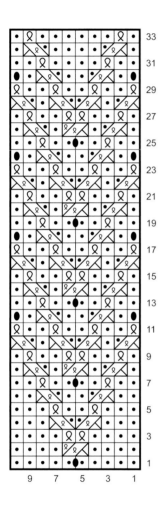

☐	Knit on RS, purl on WS.
•	Purl on RS, knit on WS.
Q	K1-tbl
•●•	Place bead between 2 purl sts as follows: p1, slide bead up close to needle, p1.
●	Place bead: slip 1 wyif, push bead up close to previous st, continue to next st. Bead sits in front of slipped st.
⧄	Slip next st to cn, hold to back, k1-tbl, k1-tbl from cn.
⧄	Slip next st to cn, hold to back, k1-tbl, p1 from cn.
⧄	Slip next st to cn, hold to front, p1, k1-tbl from cn.

HAND

Transfer sts to 4 dpns; divide evenly. Join for working in the rnd; place marker (pm) for beginning of rnd. *[Note: Needles 1 and 2 hold the sts for the back of the hand, and Needles 3 and 4 hold the sts for the palm.]*

Next Rnd: K2, M1L, [k3, M1L] 5 times, k4, M1L, [k4, M1L] 3 times, k3–46 sts.
Next Rnd: K7, pm, work Beaded Twist Stitch Chart across next 10 sts, pm, knit to end. Work even for 1 rnd.

SHAPE THUMB

Increase Rnd 1: Work 24 sts, pm for Thumb, M1L, k2, M1R, pm, knit to end–48 sts. Work even for 2 rnds.
Increase Rnd 2: Work to Thumb marker, slip marker (sm), M1L, knit to next marker, M1R, sm, knit to end–50 sts.
Repeat Increase Rnd 2 every 3 rnds 4 times–58 sts. Work even for 1 rnd.

THUMB OPENING

Next Rnd: Work 24 sts, transfer next 14 sts to waste yarn for Thumb, CO 2 sts over gap, knit to end–46 sts. Work even until Chart is complete.
Next Rnd: BO 2 sts purlwise, *slide bead up close to needle, BO next 3 sts purlwise; repeat from * to last 2 sts, slide bead up close to needle, BO remaining sts purlwise.

THUMB

Transfer sts from waste yarn to dpns, being careful not to twist sts. Rejoin yarn; pick up and knit 2 sts from sts CO over gap–16 sts. Join for working in the rnd; pm for beginning of rnd. Work even in St st for 3 rnds. BO all sts purlwise.

Left Glove

CUFF

With straight needles and Long-Tail CO, CO 52 sts. Begin St st, beginning with a WS row and slipping last st of each row purlwise. Work even for 7 rows.

Next Row (RS): K23, work first and second pleat as for Right Glove over next 24 sts, knit to end–36 sts remain.
Next Row: K2, *p1-tbl, k1; repeat from * to end.
Next Row: *P1, k1-tbl; repeat from * to last 2 sts, p2.
Repeat last 2 rows once.

HAND

Transfer sts to 4 dpns as for Right Glove. *[Note: terms for "palm" and "back of hand" are reversed.]*

Next Rnd: K3, M1L, [k4, M1L] 3 times, k5, M1L, [k3, M1L] 5 times, k1–46 sts.
Next Rnd: K29, pm, work Beaded Twist Stitch Chart across next 10 sts, pm, knit to end. Work even for 1 rnd.

SHAPE THUMB

Increase Rnd 1: K20, pm for Thumb, M1L, k2, M1R, pm, work to end–48 sts. Work even for 2 rnds.
Increase Rnd 2: Work to Thumb marker, sm, M1L, knit to next marker, M1R, sm, work to end–50 sts.
Repeat Increase Rnd 2 every 3 rnds 4 times–58 sts. Work even for 1 rnd.

THUMB OPENING

Next Rnd: K20, transfer next 14 sts to waste yarn for Thumb, CO 2 sts over gap, work to end–46 sts remain. Complete as for Right Glove.

Weave in ends. Block Gloves lightly.

Button Loops (make 2)

Using yarn with pre-strung beads and crochet
hook, work a beaded crochet chain as follows:
Make a slip knot, leaving a long tail, and place it
on crochet hook. [Slide bead up close to hook,
then holding tail end of yarn in left hand, take
hook under ball end of yarn from front to back;
draw yarn on hook back through previous st
on hook to form new st] 8 times. Fasten off and
tie tails together tightly with a square knot.

Buttons (make 2)

Tie knot in one end of 6" strand of yarn. Thread
16 beads onto yarn. Tie another knot after the last
bead, so that beads are tightly pushed together.
Tie strand of beads in a knot, then tie tails together
with a square knot.

Attach Button Loop to ribbing at wrist, so that
Loop is on back side of Glove. Attach Button
opposite Button Loop, on palm side of Glove.
Repeat for second Glove.

Weave in ends.

Brünnhilde

These opera-length gloves take their name from one of the Valkyries in the second opera, *Die Walküre*, of Wagner's Ring Cycle. The traveling twisted-stitch pattern is inspired by a beautiful German style of knitting, and the gloves are decorated with *nupps*—decorative nodes created by making five stitches out of one, then decreasing back to one stitch on the following row—which are typically used in Estonian lace. To keep the knitting stress-free, the entire hand is charted so you can easily see how the stitchwork flows.

travelling twist-stitch
nupps

SIZES

One size (to fit average woman)

FINISHED MEASUREMENTS

Approximately 7¼" circumference

YARN

Inca Gold Collection Warani (50% Suri alpaca / 50% Merino wool; 110 yards [100 meters] / 50 grams): 3 skeins #100 natural

NEEDLES

One set of five double-pointed needles (dpn) size US 6 (4 mm)
Change needle size if necessary to obtain correct gauge.

NOTIONS

Crochet hook size US C/2 (2.75 mm) (optional); stitch markers; cable needle (cn); tapestry needle; waste yarn in contrasting color

GAUGE

22 sts and 29 rnds = 4" (10 cm) in Stockinette stitch (St st)

Left Glove

FOREARM

With Long-Tail CO (see page 136), CO 55 sts, divide among 4 needles [14-14-14-13]. Join for working in the rnd, being careful not to twist sts; place marker (pm) for beginning of rnd. Begin Chart A. Work even, working decreases as indicated, until Chart is complete–35 sts remain.

WRIST AND HAND

Change to Chart B. Work even, working increases and decreases as indicated, until Rnd 80 is complete. *[Note: Be sure to reposition beginning of rnd marker on Rnds 70 and 72, as indicated in Chart Notes.]*

SHAPE THUMB

Rnd 81: Work to blue line on Chart B, pm for Thumb, change to Left Thumb Chart, work Rnd 1, pm, return to Chart B, work to end. Work even, working Thumb Chart between Thumb markers, until Rnd 96 is complete–48 sts.

Rnd 97: Work to first Thumb marker, transfer next 12 sts (8 Thumb sts and next 4 hand sts) to waste yarn for Thumb, removing Thumb markers, CO 4 sts over gap, work to end–40 sts remain. Work even until Chart B is complete. Work even in St st until piece is long enough to reach base of fingers, ending 2 sts before beginning of rnd.

DIVIDE FOR FINGERS

Redistribute sts so that last 20 sts worked are on Needle 3 for back of hand, and remaining 20 sts are on Needle 1 for palm.

[Note: Use a piece of waste yarn threaded on a tapestry needle to hold the sts for each Finger.]

Pinkie: Transfer last 5 sts from Needle 3 and first 5 sts from Needle 1 to waste yarn–10 sts.
Ring Finger: Transfer next 4 sts from each of Needles 3 and 1 to waste yarn–8 sts. **Middle Finger:** Transfer next 5 sts from each of Needles 3 and 1 to waste yarn–10 sts. **Index Finger:** Transfer remaining 6 sts from each of Needles 3 and 1 to waste yarn–12 sts.

Pinkie

Transfer sts from waste yarn to dpns. K5, CO 2 sts over gap between Pinkie and Ring Finger, k5–12 sts. Join for working in the rnd; pm for beginning of rnd. Work in St st until piece is long enough to cover Pinkie (approximately 16 rnds).

Decrease Rnd: *K2tog; repeat from * around–6 sts remain. Cut yarn, leaving a 6" tail. Draw through remaining sts, pull tight and fasten off.

Ring Finger and Middle Finger

Working one Finger at a time, transfer sts from waste yarn to dpns. Rejoin yarn; pick up and knit 2 sts from sts CO between previous Finger and current Finger, k4 for Ring Finger (k5 for Middle Finger), CO 2 sts over gap between current Finger and next Finger, k4 for Ring Finger (k5 for Middle Finger)–12 sts for Ring Finger (14 for Middle Finger). Join for working in the rnd; pm for beginning of rnd. Work in St st until piece is long enough to cover finger (approximately 20 rnds for Ring Finger; 21 rnds for Middle Finger). Complete as for Pinkie–6 sts remain for Ring Finger (7 sts for Middle Finger).

Index Finger and Thumb

Working one Finger at a time, transfer sts from waste yarn to dpns. Rejoin yarn; pick up and knit 2 sts from sts CO between previous Finger and current Finger for Index Finger (4 sts from sts CO over gap for Thumb), k12–14 sts for Index Finger (16 sts for Thumb). Join for working in the rnd; pm for beginning of rnd. Work in St st until piece is long enough to cover finger (approximately 19 rnds for Index Finger; 17 rnds for Thumb). Complete as for Pinkie–7 sts remain for Index Finger (8 sts for Thumb).

Right Glove

Work as for Left Glove to beginning of Thumb Shaping.

Shape Thumb

Rnd 81: Work to red line on Chart B, pm for Thumb, change to Right Thumb Chart, work Rnd 1, pm, return to Chart B, work to end. Work even, working Thumb Chart between Thumb markers, until Rnd 96 is complete–48 sts.

Rnd 97: Work to 4 sts before first Thumb marker, transfer next 12 sts (next 4 hand sts and 8 Thumb sts) to waste yarn for Thumb, removing Thumb markers, CO 4 sts over gap, work to end–40 sts remain. Work even in St st until piece is long enough to reach base of fingers, ending after st #15 of last rnd. Complete as for Left Glove.

Finishing

Weave in ends, using tails from rejoined yarn to close any gaps at the base of the Fingers. Block Gloves to even out sts.

KEY

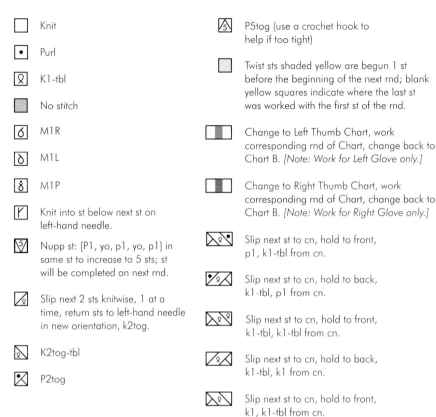

☐ Knit

• Purl

Ⓠ K1-tbl

▨ No stitch

◓ M1R

◒ M1L

⬡ M1P

⎰ Knit into st below next st on left-hand needle.

⬗ Nupp st: [P1, yo, p1, yo, p1] in same st to increase to 5 sts; st will be completed on next rnd.

⬜ Slip next 2 sts knitwise, 1 at a time, return sts to left-hand needle in new orientation, k2tog.

⬜ K2tog-tbl

⬜ P2tog

⬜ P5tog (use a crochet hook to help if too tight)

☐ Twist sts shaded yellow are begun 1 st before the beginning of the next rnd; blank yellow squares indicate where the last st was worked with the first st of the rnd.

▮ Change to Left Thumb Chart, work corresponding rnd of Chart, change back to Chart B. [Note: Work for Left Glove only.]

▮ Change to Right Thumb Chart, work corresponding rnd of Chart, change back to Chart B. [Note: Work for Right Glove only.]

⬜ Slip next st to cn, hold to front, p1, k1-tbl from cn.

⬜ Slip next st to cn, hold to back, k1-tbl, p1 from cn.

⬜ Slip next st to cn, hold to front, k1-tbl, k1-tbl from cn.

⬜ Slip next st to cn, hold to back, k1-tbl, k1 from cn.

⬜ Slip next st to cn, hold to front, k1, k1-tbl from cn.

CHART A

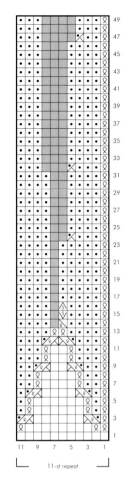

11-st repeat

CHART NOTES

1. Chart A shows one 11-st repeat (worked 5 times around), and is worked to the wrist. Chart B shows the entire rnd, and is worked from the wrist to the base of the fingers.

2. The Nupp sts in Charts A and B are worked over 2 rnds. You will increase from 1 st to 5 sts on the first rnd, then decrease back to 1 st on the following rnd. If you find it difficult to purl the 5 sts together, you might want to use a crochet hook to pull the working yarn through the sts.

3. In Chart B, there are a number of twist sts along the right-hand edge of the Chart that are shaded in yellow. These twists are begun 1 st before the beginning of the rnd. In each case, there is a corresponding yellow box at the end of the chart to indicate that the last st was worked with the first st in the next rnd. On Rnds 53, 67, and 74, once the twist has been worked, replace the beginning of rnd marker in its original position. On Rnds 70 and 72, the beginning of rnd marker will be repositioned in front of the twist sts.

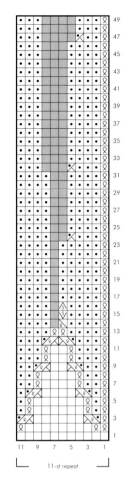

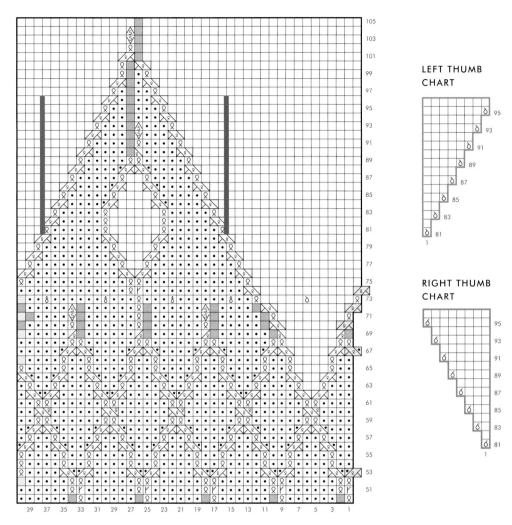

LEFT THUMB
CHART

RIGHT THUMB
CHART

4. When beginning the Thumbs, you will work a M1 between a pair of sts; these sts are indicated by a blue line for the Left Thumb and a red line for the Right Thumb. *[Note: Work the Left Thumb Chart for the Left Glove only, and the Right Thumb Chart for the Right Glove only.]* On Rnd 81 of Chart B, work to the center of the Thumb line, place marker (pm) for the beginning of the Thumb, work the first rnd of the Thumb Chart, pm for the end of the Thumb, then continue to the end of the rnd. You will continue to work increases as indicated in the Thumb Chart, until the Thumb Chart is complete. At this point, the Thumb sts will be transferred to waste yarn and set aside.

CEANGALTAS

The name of this mitten is the Irish word for bond
or tie, reflecting the nature of the knotwork design
employed. The textured tweed yarn summons
the image of rough-hewn stone, like the carved
pillars and crosses of medieval Irish sculpture. The
knotwork is formed from I-cord, which is begun
around the cuff edge, then encircles the wrist
and morphs into the knot. The split cuff and pointy
tip of the mittens are reminiscent of the shape of
armored gauntlets.

I cord edgeing, knot

Women's Small (Medium, Large)

FINISHED MEASUREMENTS
Approximately 7¼ (7¾, 8¼)"
circumference

YARN
Jo Sharp Silkroad DK Tweed (85% wool /
10% silk / 5% cashmere; 147 yards
(134 meters) / 50 grams): 2 balls #403
emerald (MC); 1 ball #400 ambrosia (A)

NEEDLES
One pair straight needles size US 5
(3.75 mm)
One set of five double-pointed needles
(dpn) size US 5 (3.75 mm)
Change needle size if necessary to obtain
correct gauge.

NOTIONS
Stitch marker; waste yarn in contrasting
color; stitch holder; straight pins

GAUGE
22 sts and 32 rnds = 4" (10 cm) in
Stockinette stitch (St st)

Right Mitten

CUFF
With straight needles and MC, CO 38 (40, 44) sts.
Begin St st beginning with a WS row. Work even
until piece measures approximately 3¼" from
the beginning, ending with a RS row, CO 2 sts at
end of last row—40 (42, 46) sts.

HAND
Transfer 2 CO sts and next 9 (10, 11) sts to Needle 1,
next 10 (11, 12) sts to Needle 2, next 10 (10, 11) sts to
Needle 3, and last 9 (9, 10) sts to Needle 4. Join for
working in the rnd, k9 (9, 10), across Needle 4; place
marker (pm) for new beginning of rnd. Slip second CO
st from Needle 1 to Needle 4. Continue in St st until
piece measures approximately 2¾" from end of Cuff.

THUMB OPENING
Next Rnd: K21 (22, 24), change to waste yarn and
k8, slip these 8 sts back to left-hand needle, change to
working yarn, knit these 8 sts again, knit to end.

Work even until piece measures approximately 6¼ (6¼,
6½)" from end of Cuff.

MITTEN TOP
Rnd 1: *K1, ssk, knit to last 3 sts of next needle, k2tog,
k1; repeat from * around—36 (38, 42) sts remain.
Rnd 2: Knit.
Repeat last 2 rnds 7 (7, 8) times—8 (10, 10) sts remain.

SIZE SMALL ONLY
Next Rnd: *K1, k2tog, k1; repeat from * around—6
sts remain. Cut yarn, leaving a 6" tail. Draw through
remaining sts, pull tight and fasten off.

to end

from I-cord

SIZE MEDIUM AND LARGE

Next Rnd: *K1, dcd, k1; repeat from *
around–6 sts remain. Cut yarn, leaving a 6" tail.
Draw through remaining sts, pull tight and
fasten off.

THUMB (ALL SIZES)

Carefully remove waste yarn from Thumb sts
and place bottom 8 sts and top 9 sts onto 2 dpns,
being careful not to twist sts. Rejoin yarn to
bottom sts, pick up and knit 2 sts at side of
Thumb Opening, knit across 8 bottom sts, pick
up and knit 2 sts at other side of Thumb Opening,
knit across 9 top sts–21 sts. Redistribute sts
evenly among 3 dpns. Join for working in the
rnd; pm for beginning of rnd.

Next Rnd: K1, k2tog, k6, ssk, k2tog, k7, ssk
(last st of this rnd together with first st of next
rnd)–17 sts remain. Work even in St st until piece
is long enough to cover thumb (approximately
18 more rnds).
Decrease Rnd: *K2tog; repeat from * to last st,
k1–9 sts remain. Cut yarn, leaving a 6" tail. Draw
through remaining sts, pull tight and fasten off.

Left Mitten

Work as for Right Mitten to Thumb Opening.

THUMB OPENING

Next Rnd: K31 (33, 37), change to waste yarn
and k8, slip these 8 sts back to left-hand needle,
change to working yarn, knit these 8 sts again,
k1. Complete as for Right Mitten.

FINISHING

Block mittens.

I-Cord Trim

With dpn and A, CO 3 sts. With WS of one
Mitten facing, beginning at side edge of Cuff
next to 2 CO sts, work 3-st Applied I-Cord (see
page 138) down side edge of Cuff, along CO
edge, then up other side edge and across 2 CO sts
where Cuff is joined, pick up and knit 1 st–4 sts.
Continue working 4-stitch I-Cord (unattached)
until unattached portion of I-Cord measures
approximately 20". Cut yarn and transfer sts to st
holder. Wrap I-Cord around wrist to center back
of hand and pin to secure. Twist I-Cord into
knotwork design as illustrated, using pins to hold
it in place as you manipulate it. Wrap end of
I-Cord around other side of wrist, back to end of
Cuff split. With A, tack down I-Cord, beginning
from the attached end and working in the same
direction in which it was wrapped, making sure that
sts do not show on RS, and that I-Cord lies flat.
Adjust length of I-Cord if necessary. Cut yarn,
leaving a 6" tail. Draw through remaining sts, pull
tight and fasten off. Sew end of I-Cord neatly
to beginning.

CHEVALIER

I think the dark bouclé yarn and the kilt straps
at the wrists of these mittens evoke a military air;
they make me think of fur-trimmed hats and
the trappings of cavalry. These mittens are also
a good example of how a knitted item can
be embellished with findings originally intended
for sewn items.

SIZES

Women's Medium (Large)

FINISHED MEASUREMENTS

Approximately 7¾ (8¼)" circumference

YARN

Garnstudio Eskimo (100% wool;
55 yards [50 meters] / 50 grams):
2 balls #14 (MC)
Garnstudio Puddel (64% mohair / 20%
wool / 16% viscose; 55 yards [50 meters]
/ 50 grams): 1 ball #8 (A)

NEEDLES

One set of five double-pointed needles
(dpn) size US 10½ (6.5 mm)
One set of five double-pointed needles
size US 11 (8 mm)
Change needle size if necessary to obtain
correct gauge.

NOTIONS

Stitch markers; waste yarn; 2 leather or
vinyl kilt straps; sewing thread and needle

GAUGE

11½ sts and 16 rnds = 4" (10 cm) in
Reverse Stockinette stitch (Rev St st) using
A and smaller needles

11½ sts and 16 rnds = 4" (10 cm) in
Stockinette stitch (St st) using MC and
larger needles

Change needle size if necessary to obtain
correct gauge.

Mittens (both alike)

CUFF

With smaller needles, Long-Tail CO (see page 136)
and A, CO 24 (26) sts, divide among 4 needles [6-6-6-6
(6-7-6-7)]. Join for working in the rnd, being careful
not to twist sts; place marker (pm) for beginning of rnd.

Rnd 1: *K1, p1; repeat from * to end. Begin Rev St st
(purl every rnd). Work even for 7 rnds.
Decrease Rnd 1: [P10 (11), p2tog] twice–22 (24) sts
remain. Work even for 7 rnds.
Decrease Rnd 2: [P9 (10), p2tog] twice–20 (22) sts
remain. Work even for 2 rnds.

HAND

Next Rnd: Change to larger needles and MC. Begin
St st (knit every rnd).
Increase Rnd: [K10 (11), M1L] twice–22 (24) sts.
Work even for 2 rnds.

SHAPE THUMB

Increase Rnd 1: K10 (11), place marker (pm) for
Thumb, M1R, k1, M1L, pm, k11 (12)–24 (26) sts.
Work even for 2 rnds.
Increase Rnd 2: Knit to marker, slip marker (sm),
M1R, k3, M1L, sm, knit to end–26 (28) sts. Work even
for 2 rnds.
Increase Rnd 3: Knit to marker, sm, M1R, k5, M1L,
sm, knit to end–28 (30) sts. Work even for 1 rnd.
Next Rnd: K10 (11), transfer next 7 sts to waste yarn
for Thumb, removing Thumb markers, CO 1 st over
gap, knit to end–22 (24) sts remain. Work even until
Mitten measures approximately 7¼ (7½)" from end of
Cuff, or until tips of fingers are just covered.
Decrease Rnd 1: *K2tog; repeat from * to end–11 (12)
sts remain.

Decrease Rnd 2: *K2tog; repeat from * to last 1 (0) st, k1 (0)–6 sts remain. Cut yarn, leaving a 6" tail. Draw tail through remaining sts, pull tight and fasten off. Weave in end.

Thumb

Transfer sts from waste yarn to larger needles. Rejoin yarn; pick up and knit 2 sts from sts CO over Thumb gap (1 st on either side)–9 sts. Divide sts among 3 needles. Join for working in the rnd; pm for beginning of rnd. Begin St st; work even until Thumb is just covered (approximately 9 rnds).

Decrease Rnd: *K2tog; repeat from * to last st, k1–5 sts remain. Cut yarn, leaving a 6" tail. Draw through remaining sts, pull tight and fasten off. Weave in end. Use tail from rejoined yarn to close any gaps around Thumb join.

Finishing

Weave in remaining ends. Choose a left and right Mitten, place palm side down with thumbs facing each other, and position a kilt strap on the back of each hand at the point where Cuff meets Hand. Make sure the end that goes through buckle points to outside of Hand. With sewing needle and thread, stitch each end of 2-part strap in place.

DRIVER

I often like to reinterpret in knitting a form
that is typically created using another method.
These fingerless gloves have the ubiquitous
leather driving glove as their inspiration.
The adjustable wristband and the knuckle
and back cutouts mimic their muse.

buckle holes

SIZES

One size (to fit average woman)

FINISHED MEASUREMENTS

Approximately 7¼" circumference

YARN

Rowan Scottish Tweed DK (100% wool;
123 yards [113 meters] / 50 grams):
1 ball #19 peat

NEEDLES

One pair straight needles size US 3
(3.25 mm)
One pair straight needles size US 4
(3.5 mm)
One set of five double-pointed needles
(dpn) size US 4 (3.5 mm)
Change needle size if necessary to obtain
correct gauge.

NOTIONS

Stitch markers; waste yarn in contrasting
color; tapestry needle; two pair 1" D-rings;
safety pins

GAUGE

22 sts and 30 rnds = 4" (10 cm)
in Stockinette stitch (St st) using
larger needles

NOTE

The ribbed Wristband at the lower edge of
the Glove is worked first, then the stitches
for the hand are picked up and knit from
the Wristband. The piece is worked flat
until the cutout on the back of the hand is
completed, then it is joined and worked
in the round. Use the Backward Loop CO
(see page 136) to CO sts over spaces—
thumbholes, fingers, knuckle cut-outs.

Wristband (make 2)

With smaller needles, CO 7 sts.
Row 1 (RS): [K1, p1] 3 times, k1.
Row 2: [P1, k1] 3 times, p1.

Repeat Rows 1 and 2 until piece measures approximately
9½" from the beginning, ending with a WS row.

SHAPE WRISTBAND

Row 1 (RS): Ssk, k1, p1, k1, k2tog–5 sts remain.
Row 2: P2, k1, p2.
Row 3: Ssk, p1, k2tog–3 sts remain.
Row 4: P1, k1, p1.
Row 5: Dcd–1 st remains. Cut yarn, leaving a 6" tail.
Draw through remaining st, pull tight and fasten off.

Right Glove

Lay Wristband flat on a table. With RS of band facing,
and pointed end of Wristband on left, place safety
pins on upper edge as follows: one pin 1¼" from right
edge (flat end), and another pin 5½" from first pin.
With larger straight needles, pick up and knit 34 sts
between pins.

Setup Row (WS): K1, p7, place marker (pm), p18,
pm for Thumb, p7, k1. [Note: Markers mark sides of
the hand.]
Row 1: K1, ssk, k4, M1R, k1, slip marker (sm), k1,
M1L, k16, M1R, k1, sm, k1, M1L, k4, k2tog, k1–36 sts.
Row 2 and all WS Rows: K1, purl to last st, k1.
Rows 3 and 5: K1, ssk, knit to last 3 sts, k2tog, k1–32
sts remain after Row 5.

Shape Thumb

Row 7: Knit to Thumb marker (first marker), sm, M1R, k2, M1L, knit to end–34 sts.

Row 9: K2, M1L, knit to Thumb marker, sm, M1R, k4, M1L, knit to last 2 sts, M1R, k2–38 sts.

Row 11: K2, M1L, knit to last 2 sts, M1R, k2–40 sts.

Row 13: K2, M1L, knit to Thumb marker, sm, M1R, k6, M1L, knit to last 2 sts, M1R, k2–44 sts.

Row 15: Knit to Thumb marker, sm, M1R, k8, M1L, knit to end, CO 2 sts–48 sts.

Redistribute sts and markers on 4 dpns for working in the rnd as follows: place last 11 sts of row on Needle 1, next 10 sts on Needle 2, next 18 sts on Needle 3, and remaining 9 sts of row on Needle 4. *[Note: Needles 4 and 1 hold the sts for the back of the hand, and Needles 2 and 3 hold the palm and Thumb sts. The marker between Needles 1 and 2 is the new beginning of rnd marker.]*

Rnd 1: Join for working in the rnd; knit to beginning of rnd marker.

Rnd 2: Knit.

Rnd 3: Knit to Thumb marker, sm, M1R, k10, M1L, knit to end–50 sts.

Rnds 4 and 5: Knit.

Rnd 6: Knit to Thumb marker, sm, M1R, k12, M1L, knit to end–52 sts.

Rnd 7: Knit.

Rnd 8: Knit to Thumb marker, slip next 14 sts to waste yarn, removing Thumb marker, CO 2 sts over gap, knit to end–40 sts remain.

Rnds 9-12: Knit.

Shape Knuckle Cutouts

Rnd 13: [K1, BO 3] 3 times, k2, BO 3, knit to end.

Rnd 14: Knit, CO 3 sts over each gap.

Rnds 15-19: Knit, removing marker after last rnd.

Divide for Fingers

Transfer all sts from Needle 4 to Needle 1 for back of hand, and all sts from Needle 3 to Needle 2 for palm–20 sts on each needle.

[Note: Use a piece of waste yarn threaded on a tapestry needle to hold the sts for each Finger.]

Pinkie: Transfer first 4 sts from Needle 1 and last 4 sts from Needle 2 to waste yarn–8 sts.

Ring Finger: Transfer next 4 sts from each of Needles 1 and 2 to waste yarn–8 sts. **Middle Finger:** Transfer next 5 sts from each of Needles 1 and 2 to waste yarn–10 sts. **Index Finger:** Transfer remaining 7 sts from each of Needles 1 and 2 to waste yarn–14 sts.

Pinkie

Transfer sts from waste yarn to dpns. K4 (back of hand sts), CO 2 sts over gap between Pinkie and Ring Finger, k4 (palm sts)–10 sts. Join for working in the rnd; pm for beginning of rnd. Knit 4 rnds. BO all sts loosely enough to fit finger through.

Ring Finger and Middle Finger

Working one Finger at a time, transfer sts from waste yarn to dpns. Rejoin yarn; pick up and knit 2 sts from sts CO between previous Finger and current Finger, k4 for Ring Finger (k5 for Middle Finger), CO 2 sts over gap between current Finger and next Finger, k4 for Ring Finger (k5 for Middle Finger)–12 sts for Ring Finger (14 sts for Middle Finger). Join for working in the rnd; pm for beginning of rnd. Knit 4 rnds for Ring Finger (5 rnds for Middle Finger). BO all sts loosely enough to fit finger though.

Index Finger and Thumb

Working one Finger at a time, transfer sts from waste yarn to dpns. Rejoin yarn; pick up and knit 2 sts from sts CO between previous Finger and current Finger (or from sts CO over gap for Thumb), k14–16 sts. Join for working in the rnd; pm for beginning of rnd. Complete as for Middle Finger.

Left Glove

Lay Wristband flat on a table. With RS of Wristband facing, and pointed end of Wristband on right, place safety pins on upper edge as follows: one pin 1¼" from left edge (flat end), and another pin 5½" from first pin. With larger straight needles, pick up and knit 34 sts between pins.

Setup Row (WS): K1, p7, pm, p18, pm, p7, k1. *[Note: Markers mark sides of the hand.]*
Row 1: K1, ssk, k4, M1R, k1, sm, k1, M1L, k16, M1R, k1, sm, k1, M1L, k4, k2tog, k1–36 sts.
Row 2 and all WS Rows: K1, p to last st, k1.
Rows 3 and 5: K1, ssk, knit to last 3 sts, k2tog, k1–32 sts after Row 5.

Shape Thumb

Row 7: Knit to 2 sts before second marker, place marker for Thumb, M1R, k2, M1L, sm, knit to end–34 sts.
Row 9: K2, M1L, knit to Thumb marker, sm, M1R, k4, M1L, sm, knit to last 2 sts, M1R, k2–38 sts.
Row 11: K2, M1L, knit to last 2 sts, M1R, k2–40 sts.
Row 13: K2, M1L, knit to Thumb marker, sm, M1R, k6, M1L, sm, knit to last 2 sts, M1R, k2–44 sts.
Row 15: Knit to Thumb marker, sm, M1R, k8, M1L, sm, knit to end, CO 2 sts–48 sts.

Redistribute sts on 4 dpns for working in the rnd as follows: place last 11 sts of row on Needle 1, next 18 sts on Needle 2, next 10 sts on Needle 3, and remaining 9 sts of row on Needle 4. *[Note: Needles 4 and 1 hold the sts for the back of the hand, and Needles 3 and 2 hold the palm and Thumb sts. The marker between Needles 1 and 2 is the new beginning of rnd marker.]*

Rnd 1: Join for working in the rnd; knit to beginning of rnd marker.

Rnd 2: Knit.

Rnd 3: Knit to Thumb marker, sm, M1R, k10, M1L–50 sts.

Rnds 4 and 5: Knit.

Rnd 6: Knit to Thumb marker, sm, M1R, k12, M1L–52 sts.

Rnd 7: Knit.

Rnd 8: Knit to thumb marker, slip next 14 sts to waste yarn, removing Thumb marker, CO 2 sts over gap and join to beginning of rnd–40 sts.

Rnds 9-12: Knit.

SHAPE KNUCKLE CUTOUTS

Rnd 13: K3, BO 3, k2, [BO 3, k1] 3 times, knit to end.

Rnd 14: Knit, CO 3 sts over each gap.

Rnds 15-19: Knit, removing marker after last rnd.

DIVIDE FOR FINGERS

Work as for Right Glove, reversing order of Fingers, beginning with Index Finger and working Thumb last.

FINISHING

Use tails from rejoined yarns to close any holes around Fingers and Thumb. Weave in ends. With WS of Wristband facing, place flat sections of one pair of D-rings on flat end of Wristband. Fold end to WS and sew in place, being careful not to let sts show on RS. Repeat for other Glove.

Evening Light

In the beaded versions of these fingerless gloves, the metallic beads glimmer softly against the dark colors of the variegated yarn, like stars that begin to appear in the sky at dusk. The "plain" versions are worked without beads and can be machine washed (as long as you use machine-washable yarn). All of these gloves are worked from side to side in Garter stitch, like the pulse-warmers of Norway, but with a short-rowed thumb gore, so they can be worn higher on the hand than the pulse-warmers.

short row thumb gore

Sizes

Children's (Women's Medium short length, Women's Large short length, Women's Medium long length, Women's Large long length, Men's Medium, Men's Large)

Finished Measurements

Approximately 5½ (6, 6½, 6, 6½, 8, 9)" circumference; approximately 5 (5¾, 5¾, 8¼, 8¼, 7, 7½)" long

Note: Glove stretches appreciably when worn.

Yarn

Mountain Colors Bearfoot (60% superwash wool / 25% mohair / 15% nylon; 350 yards [318 meters] / 100 grams): 1 hank all sizes. Children's version shown in rich red; Women's short length shown in elderberry; Women's long length shown in juniper; and Men's version shown in bark brown.

Needles

One pair straight needles size US 4 (3.5 mm)
One straight or double-pointed needle (dpn) size US 4 (3.5 mm), for Three-Needle BO
Change needle size if necessary to obtain correct gauge.

Notions

Stitch marker; removable marker; stitch holder. For Women's Versions only: 250 size 6/0 beads; wire beading needle; needle-nose pliers (for crushing off misshapen beads)

Gauge

24 sts and 48 rows = 4" (10 cm) in Garter stitch (knit every row)

Notes

Beaded (Women's) Versions Only: Beads are placed on WS rows, between sts, so that they show on the RS. Note that charts show WS rows only, and should be followed from left to right. RS rows are not charted, as they are plain; knit all RS rows.

Slip first st of every row purlwise with yarn in front (do this at thumb edge also). The slipped st will be included in the st count, but will not be mentioned in the instructions.

If you would like to make the Women's versions omitting the beads, simply work the appropriate number of plain rows in place of the charts

Three-Needle BO

Place the stitches to be joined onto two same-size needles; hold the pieces to be joined with the right sides facing each other and the needles parallel, both pointing to the right. Holding both needles in your left hand, using working yarn and a third needle the same size or one size larger, insert the third needle into the first stitch on the front needle, then into the first stitch on the back needle; knit these two stitches together; *knit the next st from each needle together (you now have two stitches on the right-hand needle); pass the first stitch over the second stitch to BO 1 stitch. Repeat from * until 1 stitch remains on the third needle. Cut the yarn, leaving a 6" tail. Draw through the remaining st, pull tight and fasten off.

Prepare Beads

Thread yarn through wire beading needle. Thread beads onto yarn, adding a few extra beads in case you find any that are misshapen and must be crushed off. For more information, see page 135.

Left Glove

With Long-Tail CO (see page 136), CO 30 (35, 35, 50, 50, 42, 45) sts, leaving a very long tail. Begin Garter st (knit every row), slipping first st of every row purlwise wyif. Work even for 33 (35, 39, 0, 2, 49, 55) rows.

WOMEN'S MEDIUM LONG LENGTH, WOMEN'S LARGE LONG LENGTH ONLY

Begin Chart

Next Row (WS): Work Long Version Chart across 25 sts, working Chart from left to right, place marker (pm), knit to end. Work even until Chart is complete, knitting all RS rows and ending with a WS row. Work even for 0 (2) rows.

ALL SIZES

Short Row Thumb Shaping

Rows 1 (RS) and 2: Work 9 (11, 11, 11, 11, 14, 15) sts and place on holder, k4, wrp-t, knit to end–21 (24, 24, 39, 39, 28, 30) sts remain. Place removable marker on Row 1 to indicate RS of work.
Rows 3 and 4: Work 6 sts, wrp-t, knit to end.
Rows 5 and 6: Work 8 sts, wrp-t, knit to end.
Rows 7 and 8: Work 10 sts, wrp-t, knit to end.

ALL ADULT SIZES ONLY
Rows 9 and 10: Work 12 sts, wrp-t, knit to end.

MEN'S SIZES ONLY
Rows 11 and 12: Work 14 sts, wrp-t, knit to end.

MEN'S SIZE LARGE ONLY
Rows 13 and 14: Work 16 sts, wrp-t, knit to end.

ALL SIZES
Next 2 Rows: Knit across all 21 (24, 24, 39, 39, 28, 30) sts. Repeat Rows 8-3 (10-3, 10-3, 10-3, 10-3, 12-3, 14-3), working rows in reverse order.
Next 2 Rows: Work 4 sts, wrp-t, knit to end, knit across sts from holder–30 (35, 35, 50, 50, 42, 45) sts. Work even for 32 (5, 7, 1, 3, 48, 54) rows, ending with a WS (RS, RS, RS, RS, WS, WS) row.

WOMEN'S MEDIUM SHORT LENGTH, WOMEN'S LARGE SHORT LENGTH ONLY

Begin Chart

Next Row (WS): Work Short Version Chart across 32 sts, working Chart from left to right, pm, work to end. Work even until Chart is complete, knitting all RS rows and ending with a WS row, removing marker on last row. Work even for 4 (6) rows.

WOMEN'S MEDIUM LONG LENGTH, WOMEN'S LARGE LONG LENGTH ONLY
Work entire Long Version Chart again.
Next Row (RS): Work even for 0 (2) rows.

ALL SIZES
Leave sts on needle; do not cut yarn.

Join Side Seam

With RS facing, using separate needle, pick up and knit 29 (34, 34, 49, 49, 41, 44) sts from CO row, using tail from CO. Fold Glove so that RS's are together, and join live sts and picked-up sts using Three-Needle BO (see page 56).

Right Glove

ALL SIZES EXCEPT WOMEN'S MEDIUM SHORT LENGTH AND WOMEN'S LARGE SHORT LENGTH
Work as for Left Glove.

WOMEN'S MEDIUM SHORT LENGTH, WOMEN'S LARGE SHORT LENGTH ONLY
With Long-Tail CO, CO 35 sts, leaving a very long tail. Begin Garter st, slipping first st of every row purlwise wyif. Work even for 4 (6) rows.

Begin Chart

Next Row (WS): Work Women's Short Version Chart as for Left Glove until Chart is complete. Work even for 4 (6) rows.
Work Short Row Thumb Shaping as for Left Glove. Work even for 34 (38) rows. Leave sts on needle; do not cut yarn. Join Side Seam as for Left Glove.

KEY

• Knit on WS.

⩔ Slip st purlwise wyif.

●• Slip bead up close to needle, then k1.

Note: Charts show WS rows only.
Knit all RS rows, slipping first st wyif.

Knitting with beads is easy; after you have made a pair of these, consider designing your own beading pattern on a piece of graph paper. Use the number of rows given in this pattern as a guideline, then sketch a design on the paper, and draw dots to represent beads along the lines of your sketch.

SHORT VERSION CHART

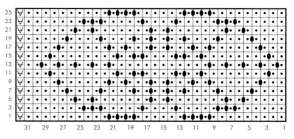

LONG VERSION CHART

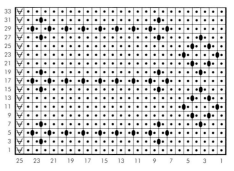

FILIGREE

These fingerless gloves, worked in an interestingly textured cotton yarn, have a casual insouciance that makes them an ideal accessory for jeans, beachwear, clubwear—anything. These gloves are available in two different lengths (for long version, see left; for shorter version, see page 63), and the stitch pattern is reminiscent of the twisted wirework of filigreed jewelry. The gloves are worked in the round to the thumbhole, then worked flat for one pattern repeat, then rejoined into a round and completed. A bit of closed blanket stitch finishes the thumbhole.

Stitch pattern

Women's Small/Medium (Large)

FINISHED MEASUREMENTS
Approximately 6½ (7¼)" circumference,
unstretched. *Note: Glove will stretch
appreciably when worn.*
Wrist-Length Version: Approximately
6" long
Elbow-Length Version: Approximately
11¼" long

YARN
Nashua Handknits Creative Focus Cotton
(100% cotton; 93 yards [85 meters] /
50 grams): Wrist-Length Version: 1 (2)
balls #027 McDearis Moors; Elbow-Length
Version: 2 (3) balls #10 passion

NEEDLES
One set of five double-pointed needles
(dpn) size US 6 (4 mm)
Change needle size if necessary to obtain
correct gauge.

NOTIONS
Stitch marker

GAUGE
20 sts and 24 rows = 4" (10 cm) in
Openwork Pattern

NOTES
There are two versions of the Openwork Pattern used
in this pattern; one for working in the round and one
for working back and forth. Be sure to use the version
specified in the text.

To work a yo at the beginning of a row before a purl st,
wrap yarn over right-hand needle from front to back,
then between needles to front again, ready to purl
the next stitch.

STITCH PATTERN
Openwork Pattern in-the-Rnd
(multiple of 4 sts; 4-rnd repeat)
Rnd 1: Knit, wrapping yarn around needle twice
for each st.
Rnd 2: *Slip next 4 sts to right-hand needle, dropping
extra wraps, slip them back to left-hand needle, then
k4tog, p4tog into these 4 sts; repeat from * to end.
*[Note: Stitch count will be half of original number after
this rnd.]*
Rnd 3: *K1, yo; repeat from * to end. *[Note: Original
stitch count restored.]*
Rnd 4: Knit.
Repeat Rnds 1-4 for Openwork Pattern in-the-Rnd.

Openwork Pattern
(multiple of 4 sts; 4-row repeat)
Row 1 (WS): Purl, wrapping yarn around needle twice
for each st.
Row 2: *Slip next 4 sts to right-hand needle, dropping
extra wraps, slip them back to left-hand needle, then
k4tog, p4tog into these 4 sts; repeat from * to end.
*[Note: Stitch count will be half of original number after
this row.]*
Row 3: *Yo, p1; repeat from * to end. *[Note: Original
stitch count restored.]*
Row 4: Knit.
Repeat Rows 1-4 for Openwork Pattern.

Fingerless Gloves (both alike)

WRIST
With Long-Tail CO (see page 136), CO 32 (36) sts, divide evenly among 4 needles [8-8-8-8 (8-8-8-12)]. Join for working in the rnd, being careful not to twist sts; place marker (pm) for beginning of rnd. Purl 1 rnd. Knit 1 rnd. Purl 1 rnd.

Change to Openwork Pattern in-the-Rnd; work even for 16 rnds for Wrist-Length Version [48 rnds for Elbow-Length Version].

THUMB OPENING
Change to Openwork Pattern, dropping beginning of rnd marker; working back and forth, work even for 4 rows.

PALM
Change to Openwork Pattern in-the-Rnd. Join for working in the rnd; pm for beginning of rnd. Work even for 8 rnds. Purl 1 rnd. Knit 1 rnd. Purl 1 rnd. BO all sts knitwise.

FINISHING
Using Closed Blanket Stitch (see page 136), sew around each thumb hole. Weave in ends.

GLAISTIG

These fingerless gloves are worked in an
old English lace pattern (collected by
Barbara G. Walker in her phenomenal book
A Treasury of Knitting Patterns) and embellished
with a picot bind-off. The ribbed cuffs are
worked from side to side, and a yarn-covered
buckle is sewn to the end of each one. The
gloves are named for a beautiful unearthly
being from Scottish lore who dwells near water,
and happens to be part goat (a pun on the
cashmere content of the yarn).

stitch pattern

covered buckle

FINISHED MEASUREMENTS
Approximately 7½" circumference

YARN
Inca Gold Collection Baby Silk Cashmere (70% baby alpaca / 20% silk / 10% cashmere; 219 yards [200 meters] / 50 grams): 1 ball #1340 leaf green

NEEDLES
One pair straight needles size US 4 (3.5 mm)
Change needle size if necessary to obtain correct gauge.

NOTIONS
Tapestry needle; two plastic center-bar buckles with 1¼" (33 mm) inside diameter

GAUGE
20 sts and 32 rows = 4" (10 cm) in English Mesh Lace from Chart

NOTE
Knitted CO
You may use this method for your initial cast-on, or add stitches at the beginning of a row. When working an initial cast-on, make a slip knot and place it on the left-hand needle. *Knit the first stitch on the left-hand needle, draw up a new loop but do not drop the old loop from the left-hand needle, place the new loop on the left-hand needle. Repeat from * until the required number of stitches have been cast on.

Cuffs (make 2)
With Long-Tail CO (see page 136), CO 24 sts, leaving a long tail.
Row 1 (WS): P1, *p2, k2; repeat from * to last 3 sts, p2, slip 1 purlwise wyif.
Row 2: K1, *k2, p2; repeat from * to last 3 sts, k2, slip 1 purlwise wyib.
Repeat Rows 1 and 2 until piece measures approximately 9½" from the beginning, ending with a WS row.
BO all sts in pattern.

Fingerless Gloves (both alike)
With Long-Tail CO, CO 39 sts. Purl 1 row.
Next Row (RS): Begin English Mesh Lace Chart. Work even until piece measures approximately 5" from the beginning, ending with a WS row.
Picot BO: BO 3 sts, *slip 1 st from right-hand needle back to left-hand needle, CO 2 sts using the Knitted CO, BO next 5 sts; repeat from * to end.

FINISHING
Block Glove pieces to approximately 7½" wide by 5" long. Do not block Cuffs. Sew side seams of Gloves for 2" up from CO edge, and for 1¼" down from BO edge, leaving approximately 1¾" open for thumb.

Self-Covered Buckle (make 2)
Cut a strand of yarn approximately 2 yards (1.8 meters) long. Fold in half and thread the two ends through a tapestry needle. To begin, fix strand to buckle by threading two free ends through loop at end of your doubled strand, around outer circle of buckle. Continue in Closed Blanket Stitch (see page 136) with doubled strand, packing sts very densely and tightly around outer circle of buckle, and cutting additional lengths of yarn as needed. Weave in ends on back of buckle. If desired, add a small dab of white glue where outer circle meets the center bar, and push yarn wraps together over any plastic that is showing. Using CO tail, sew buckle to CO edge of each Cuff by folding end of Cuff over center bar of buckle and stitching neatly on WS, making sure sts do not show on RS.

ENGLISH MESH LACE CHART

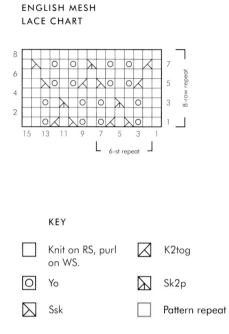

KEY

□	Knit on RS, purl on WS.	⊠	K2tog
Ⓞ	Yo	◩	Sk2p
◺	Ssk	□	Pattern repeat

Measure approximately 6½" (or your wrist circumference) from center of buckle and place marker. Position Cuff on Glove so that buckle is centered on back of hand. Cuff should wrap around wrist, thread through buckle and point to heel of hand, away from thumb. Making sure not to sew too tightly, sew Cuff to lower edge of Glove, from buckle to marker, easing in fullness of Glove, and ending approximately ¼" before reaching buckle again. Weave in ends.

GOLDEN BRACELETS

The Fair Isle band at the wrist of these gloves
is designed to emulate the appearance of golden
bracelets. The motif is inspired by the intricate
curvilinear shapes that decorated early medieval
Celtic jewelry. The cuff below the bracelet is
subtly flared and has a picot edge. The gloves
are worked in a fine Shetland wool, whose subtle
heathering blends the various colors into the
appearance of time-burnished gold.

picot-hem edge

One size (to fit average woman)

FINISHED MEASUREMENTS
Approximately 7½" circumference

YARN
Jamieson's Shetland Spindrift (100% pure
Shetland wool; 115 yards [105 meters]
/ 25 grams): 2 balls #140 rye (MC);
1 ball each #232 blue lovat (A), #233
spagnum (B), #1160 scotch broom (C),
and #429 old gold (D)

NEEDLES
One set of five double-pointed needles
(dpn) size US 1½ (2.5 mm)
One set of five double-pointed needles
size US 2 (2.75 mm)
Change needle size if necessary to obtain
correct gauge.

NOTIONS
Stitch markers; waste yarn in contrasting
color (or use A, B, C, or D); tapestry needle

GAUGE
32 sts and 44 rnds = 4" (10 cm) in
Stockinette stitch (St st) using
smaller needles

16 sts and 16 rnds = 2" (5 cm)
in Stockinette stitch over Fair Isle
Chart using larger needles

Left Glove

With smaller needles, Long-Tail CO (see page 136)
and MC, CO 64 sts, divide evenly among 4 needles
[16-16-16-16]. Join for working in the rnd, being
careful not to twist sts; place marker (pm) for beginning
of rnd. *[Note: Needles 1 and 2 hold the sts for the palm
and Thumb, and Needles 3 and 4 hold the sts for the
back of the hand.]* Begin St st. Work even for 7 rnds.

Picot Rnd: *K2tog, yo; repeat from * around.
Next Rnd: Change to St st; work even for 14 rnds.
Decrease Rnd: *K14, k2tog; repeat from * around–60
sts remain.

BEGIN CHART
Next Rnd: Change to larger needles. Begin Fair Isle
Chart. Work even until Chart is complete, carrying
colors not in use loosely up WS at beginning of Chart.
Next Rnd: Change to smaller needles, MC, and St st.
Work even for 4 rnds.

SHAPE THUMB
Increase Rnd 1: K28, pm for Thumb, M1L, k2, M1R,
pm, knit to end–62 sts. Work even for 2 rnds.
Increase Rnd 2: Knit to first marker, M1L, knit to
second marker, M1R, knit to end–64 sts. Work even for
2 rnds.
Repeat last 3 rnds 6 times, then repeat Increase Rnd 2
once–78 sts. Work even for 1 rnd.

Next Rnd: Knit to first marker, transfer next 20 sts
to waste yarn for Thumb, CO 2 sts over gap, knit
to end–60 sts remain. Work even in St st until piece is
long enough to reach base of Pinkie (approximately
13 rnds), ending 7 sts before end of last rnd, removing
all markers on last rnd.

Divide for Fingers

Pinkie: Transfer next 14 sts [last 7 sts of rnd and first 7 sts of next rnd] to waste yarn, pm, CO 2 sts over gap, knit to 7 sts before marker.

Ring Finger: Transfer next 16 sts [7 sts from back, 2 CO sts from previous rnd, and 7 sts from palm] to waste yarn, removing marker, pm, CO 2 sts over gap, knit to 7 sts before marker.

Middle Finger: Transfer next 16 sts [7 sts from back, 2 CO sts from previous rnd, and 7 sts from palm] to waste yarn, removing marker, pm, CO 2 sts over gap–20 sts remain for Index Finger.

Index Finger

Work in St st until piece is long enough to cover index finger (approximately 29 rnds).

Decrease Rnd: *K2tog; repeat from * around–10 sts remain. Cut yarn, leaving a 6" tail. Draw through remaining sts, pull tight and fasten off, with tail to the inside.

Middle, Ring, and Pinkie Fingers, and Thumb

Working one Finger at a time, transfer sts from waste yarn to dpns. Rejoin MC; pick up and knit 2 sts from sts CO between previous Finger and current Finger (or from sts CO over gap for Thumb), knit to end–18 sts for Middle Finger [18 sts for Ring Finger; 16 sts for Pinkie; 22 sts for Thumb]. Join for working in the rnd; pm for beginning of rnd. Work in St st until piece is long enough to cover finger (approximately 36 rnds for Middle Finger, 32 rnds for Ring Finger, 25 rnds for Pinkie, and 25 rnds for Thumb). Complete as for Index Finger–9 sts remain for Middle Finger [9 sts for Ring Finger; 8 sts for Pinkie; 11 sts for Thumb].

Right Glove

Work as for Left Glove to beginning of Thumb Shaping. [*Note: Terms for "back of hand" and "palm" should be reversed.*]

FAIR ISLE CHART

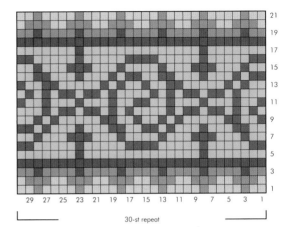

30-st repeat

KEY

▢ Knit with MC.

▨ Knit with A.

▨ Knit with B.

▨ Knit with C.

▨ Knit with D.

Shape Thumb

Increase Rnd 1: K30, pm, M1L, k2, M1R, pm, knit to end–62 sts. Complete as for Left Glove, working Fingers in the same order.

Finishing

Block Gloves. Fold facings under at picot rnd and neatly sew to WS, being careful not to let sts show on RS. Weave in remaining ends.

Gothic

These sequined hand warmers evoke the angular structure of Gothic architecture. The flared cuff is attenuated by twisted ribbing at the wrist, and the back of the hand tapers gently to a point. The last three stitches on the back of the hand are worked in I-cord, which is formed into a loop and circles the middle finger. The sequined decoration and elegant shape make them appropriate for formal occasions, but they also look great in more casual settings. Wear them also if your hands get cold while working at a computer; the shape does not impede the movement of your hands while typing.

twisted ribbing
edging

Sizes

One size (to fit average woman)

Finished Measurements

Approximately 8" cuff circumference,
6¾" wrist circumference

Yarn

Rowan Yarns Kid Classic (70% lambswool/
26% kid mohair / 4% nylon;
151 yards [140 meters] / 50 grams):
1 ball #828 feather

Needles

One set of five double-pointed needles
(dpn) size US 6 (4 mm)
One set of five double-pointed needles
size US 7 (4.5 mm)
Change needle size if necessary to obtain
correct gauge.

Notions

Stitch marker; 20 coordinating sequins;
sewing needle and thread

Gauge

20 sts and 28 rnds = 4" (10 cm) in
Stockinette stitch (St st) using larger needles

Note

Channel Island CO

This is an unusual cast-on, which, in addition
to being strong, also makes a very decorative
edging. First, cut a piece of yarn a bit longer
than the length you would normally use for the
Long-Tail CO. Pull another long length from
the ball to be left for the tail; do NOT cut it.
Holding both strands together, make a slip knot
of both strands, about 6" from the end of the
cut strand nearest to the ball, and put it on the
right-hand needle, with the two long tails hanging
to the front of the needle, and the end attached
to the ball and the short end of the cut strand to the back.
Hold the two tails in your left hand and the ball strand in
your right hand (disregard the short end of the cut strand).
*Wrap the double tail twice around your left thumb coun-
terclockwise (opposite from Long-Tail CO), bring the ball
strand under the needle and over the top to the back to
create a yarnover, and hold it in your right hand, insert the
needle into both wraps on your thumb, and with the ball
strand, wrap the yarn around the needle as if to knit, draw
the loop through the thumb wraps, and pull them gently to
tighten. You have just cast on two stitches. Repeat from *
until the required number of stitches have been cast on.

Hand Warmers (both alike)

With larger needles and Channel Island CO, CO 39 sts.
Divide sts among larger dpns [9-10-10-10]. Join for
working in the rnd, being careful not to twist sts; place
marker (pm) for beginning of rnd.

Next Rnd: Purl into each loop of slipknot at beginning
of CO to increase 1 st, purl to end–40 sts.
Next Rnd: Begin St st. Work even for 17 rnds.
Decrease Rnd: K5, k2tog, k4, k2tog, [k5, k2tog] twice,
k4, k2tog, k5, k2tog–34 sts remain.
Next Rnd: Change to smaller dpns. *K1-tbl, p1; repeat
from * to end. Repeat last rnd 4 times.

Next Rnd: Change to larger dpns and St st. Work even
for 4 rnds.
Next Rnd: BO 17 sts, knit to end–17 sts remain.
Next Row (WS): Change to working back and forth.
P1, k1, purl to last 2 sts, k1, p1.
Next Row: Begin Diamond Chart. Work Rows 1-15,
working decreases as indicated in Chart–3 sts remain.
Do NOT turn work after last row.

Next Row (RS): Change to I-Cord (see page 138). Work even until I-Cord measures approximately 2½". Cut yarn, leaving a 6" tail. Draw through remaining sts, pull tight and fasten off. Using tail, sew end of I-Cord to WS at beginning of I-Cord to make a small loop, being careful not to let sts show on RS.

FINISHING

Weave in ends. Block Hand Warmers. Sew sequins in the "window" created inside the twist-stitch motif on Rows 4–8 of the chart. (See photo, page 72).

DIAMOND CHART

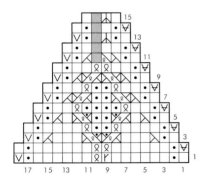

KEY

☐ Knit on RS, purl on WS.

• Purl on RS, knit on WS.

⑆ Slip 1 st purlwise with yarn in back.

⑆ Slip 1 st purlwise with yarn in front.

▨ No stitch

⑂ Knit into st below next st on left-hand needle.

⑆ K1-tbl on RS, p1-tbl on WS.

⑆ Ssk

⑆ K2tog

⑆ K2tog-tbl

⑆ Double centered decrease:
Slip next 2 sts together knitwise to right-hand needle, k1, pass 2 slipped sts over knit st.

⑆ Slip 1 st purlwise, slip 1 st knitwise, return slipped sts back to left-hand needle in new orientations, k2tog these 2 sts, but do not drop sts from left-hand needle, purl first st, slip both sts from left-hand needle together.

⑆ Purl into back of second st, but do not drop st from left-hand needle, k2tog-tbl first 2 sts, slip both sts from left-hand needle together.

⑆ Slip 1 st purlwise, slip 1 st knitwise, return slipped sts back to left-hand needle in new orientations, k2tog these 2 sts, but do not drop sts from left-hand needle, insert right-hand needle between 2 sts just worked and knit first st again, slip both sts from left-hand needle together.

⑆ Knit into back of second st, then knit first and second sts together through back loops, slip both sts from left-hand needle together.

GRETEL

Icelandic wool is one of my favorite kinds of yarn,
especially for weather-proof accessories. I love
the rusticity, the colors (especially the heathers), the
combination of water-repelling guard hairs and
soft, warm undercoat fibers, and the history—the
sheep in Iceland today are descendants of those
brought there by Vikings over a thousand years ago.
These mittens are knit flat, with an extra strand
of a lighter-weight yarn held along with the working
yarn on the palm side to create a reinforced palm.
The lighter-weight yarn is also used for the side gore,
and for the decorative embroidery and edging.
Use your imagination with the needle-felted motif:
the single-ply yarn can be used to "draw" any
design on the mittens.

SIZES

One size (to fit average woman)

FINISHED MEASUREMENTS

Approximately 8¼" circumference

YARN

Reynolds Lopi (100% Icelandic wool; 110 yards [100 meters] / 100 grams): 1 ball #9971 amber heather (MC)

Reynolds Lite-Lopi (100% Icelandic wool; 110 yards [100 meters] / 50 grams): 1 ball #1401 hazel heather (A)

NEEDLES

One pair straight needles size US 10½ (6.5 mm)
One pair straight needles size US 8 (5 mm)
One set of five double-pointed needles (dpn) size US 10½ (6.5 mm)
One set of five double-pointed needles size US 8 (5 mm)
Change needle size if necessary to obtain correct gauge.

NOTIONS

Stitch markers; waste yarn in contrasting color; tapestry needle; 4"x4" piece of tightly woven cloth; sewing pins; six ¾" wood buttons; sewing needle and thread; felting needle

GAUGE

12 sts and 18 rows = 4" (10 cm) in Stockinette stitch (St st) using larger needles and MC

NOTE

Needle Felting

A felting needle is a thin triangular or star-shaped needle with barbs all over the tip. You can use it to apply fleece or pieces of woolen yarn with low twist (any single which you can untwist gently and see the fibers from which it was spun). When you stab the needle through the appliqué and into the base, the barbs push the fibers of the appliqué into the fibers of the base, but it pulls out cleanly so they stay there. Repeated stabbing eventually mixes the two layers so much that the appliqué stays in place. If you turn it over to the wrong side, you will be able to see the color of the appliqué coming through the base. This method can be used to "draw" onto an item with yarn.

Left Mitten

With larger straight needles and MC, CO 26 sts. Begin St st, beginning with a WS row. Work even for 11 rows.

PALM REINFORCEMENT

Row 1 (RS): K1, place marker (pm), change to 1 strand each of MC and A held together, k11, drop A, pm, knit to end.
Row 2: Purl to marker, change to 1 strand each of MC and A held together, p11, drop A, p1. Work even in St st for 8 rows.

THUMB OPENING

Next Row (RS): Work 8 sts, change to waste yarn and k4, slip these 4 sts back to left-hand needle, change to working yarn, knit these 4 sts again, work to end. Work even until piece measures approximately 8½" from the beginning, ending with a WS row. Cut A.

SHAPE MITTEN TOP

Row 1 (RS): Continuing with MC only, k1, *k2, k2tog; repeat from * to last st, k1–20 sts remain.
Rows 2 and 4: Purl.
Row 3: K1, *k1, k2tog; repeat from * to last st, k1–14 sts remain.
Row 5: K1, *k2tog; repeat from * to last st, k1–8 sts remain. Cut yarn, leaving a 6" tail. Draw through remaining sts, pull tight and fasten off.

THUMB

Carefully remove waste yarn from Thumb sts and place bottom 4 sts and top 5 sts onto 2 larger dpns. Rejoin MC and A, and with 1 strand of each held together, pick up and knit 1 st at side of Thumb Opening, knit across 4 bottom sts, pick up and knit 1 st at other side of Thumb Opening, knit across 5 top sts–11 sts. Distribute sts among 3 dpns. Join for working in the rnd; pm for beginning of rnd.
Next Rnd: K2tog, k2, ssk, k5–9 sts remain. Work even until piece is long enough to cover thumb (approximately 9 more rnds).
Next Rnd: *K2tog; repeat from * to last st, k1–5 sts remain. Cut yarns, leaving 6" tails. Draw through remaining sts, pull tight and fasten off, with tail to the inside.

Right Mitten

Work as for Left Mitten to beginning of Palm Reinforcement.

Row 1 (RS): K14, pm, change to 1 strand each of MC and A held together, k11, drop A, pm, k1.

Row 2: P1, change to 1 strand each of MC and A held together, p11, drop A, purl to end. Work even in St st for 8 rows.

Thumb Opening

Next row (RS): Work 14 sts, change to waste yarn and k4, slip these 4 sts back to left-hand needle, change to working yarn, knit these 4 sts again, work to end. Work even until piece measures approximately 8½" from the beginning, ending with a WS row. Cut A. Complete as for Left Mitten.

Finishing

Side Gore

With RS facing, smaller straight needles and A, beginning at top of Mitten and working one half stitch in from edge, pick up and knit 42 sts down side edge of Mitten (edge of *back* of hand for Left Mitten, edge of *palm* of hand for Right Mitten).

Short Row Shaping (see page 140)

Rows 1 (WS) and 2: P11, wrp-t, knit to end.

Rows 3 and 4: P11, purl next st together with wrap, p10, wrp-t, knit to end.

Rows 5 and 6: P22, purl next st together with wrap, p9, wrp-t, knit to end.

Row 7: P32, purl next st together with wrap, purl to end.

Row 8: Knit to end.

BO all sts purlwise, leaving a very long tail. Using tail, sew BO edge to other side edge of Mitten, working one half stitch in from edge.

Decoration

Place cloth inside Mitten to prevent felting needle from going through all layers. Cut strand of A, lay it on center back of Mitten and twist it into shape shown in illustration. Anchor it with pins if you like, then begin punching felting needle through yarn and Mitten. Begin with a few jabs at

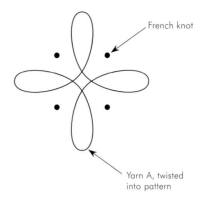

French knot

Yarn A, twisted into pattern

each crossover point until shape is set as desired, then continue jabbing over whole strand until it is embedded in Mitten fabric. Cut any extra off strand, and felt in ends with needle. With A threaded on tapestry needle, make 4 French Knots (see page 137) as shown in illustration.

I-Cord Edging

With 2 smaller dpns and A, CO 4 sts. With WS facing, beginning and ending at outside edges of Gore, work Applied I-Cord (see page 138) around lower edge of Mitten. Cut yarn, leaving a 6" tail. Draw through remaining sts, pull tight and fasten off.

With sewing needle and thread, sew 3 buttons to side edges of each Mitten, one approximately 2½" up from lower edge, one approximately 2" down from top of Mitten, and one spaced in between. Sew buttons on so that Mitten edges are gathered together over Gore; do not sew through Gore.

Weave in ends.

HOUNDSTOOTH MISCELLANY

These arm warmers feature a composition
of three different patterns: houndstooth
in two sizes and a herringbone pattern. The
colorwork pattern is reminiscent of rustic
tweedy cloth; but worked in this wool/alpaca
blend yarn, it has a subtle chiaroscuro
haze from the long fibers. The arm warmers
are worked flat, and edged with a crab
stitch crocheted edging. The suede lacing
instills the design with an equestrian quality.

SIZES

One size (to fit average woman)

FINISHED MEASUREMENTS

Approximately 5½" wrist circumference;
approximately 9" forearm circumference;
approximately 8¼" long, including edging
*Note: Since Arm Warmer laces up,
circumference measurements are adjustable.*

YARN

Nashua Handknits Creative Focus Worsted
(75% wool / 25% alpaca; 220 yards
[201 meters] / 100 grams): 1 ball each
#0410 espresso (MC) and #2120
brick (A)

NEEDLES

One pair straight needles size US 7 (4.5 mm)
Change needle size if necessary to obtain
correct gauge.

NOTIONS

Crochet hook size US 7 (4.5 mm); 3½ yards
(3 meters) suede cord

GAUGE

22 sts and 22 rows = 4" (10 cm) in
Stockinette stitch (St st) over
Houndstooth Chart

ARM WARMERS (BOTH ALIKE)

With MC and Long-Tail CO (see page 136), CO 30 sts.
Purl 1 row.
Next Row (RS): Begin Houndstooth Chart. Work
even, working increases as indicated in Chart, until
Chart is completed–50 sts. Cut A. BO all sts purlwise.

FINISHING

Block pieces to measurements. With RS facing, using
crochet hook and MC, beginning at lower right-hand
corner of Arm Warmer, work Crab Stitch Edging
around entire piece.

Crab Stitch Edging

Row 1 (Single Crochet): Work from right to left
for right-handers, or from left to right for left-handers.
Make slipknot and place on hook. *Insert hook into
next st (along lower or upper edge) or between two
rows (side edges). Yo hook, pull through to RS–2 loops
on hook. Yo hook, draw through both loops–1 loop on
hook. Repeat from * to end. *[Note: It may be necessary
to skip a row every so often when working along a side
edge, in order to prevent puckering.]*
Row 2 (Reverse Single Crochet): Work from left
to right for right-handers, or from right to left for
left-handers. *Insert hook into previous single crochet,
yo hook, pull through to RS–2 loops on hook. Yo
hook, draw through both loops–1 loop on hook. Repeat
from * to end. Fasten off.

Cut 60" (1.5 meter) length of suede cord and lace
through gaps in Row 2 of Crab Stitch Edging in a criss-
cross fashion, working from wrist edge to forearm edge.
Knot at top of Arm Warmer and trim to desired length.

Weave in ends.

HOUNDSTOOTH CHART

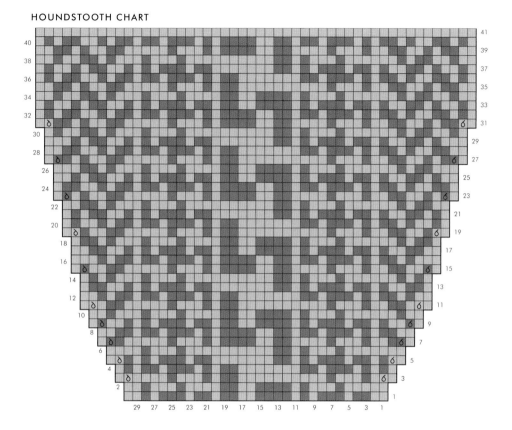

KEY

☐	Knit on RS, purl on WS.
☐	MC
■	A
◌	M1L
◌	M1R

Jack-in-the-Box

These flip-top mittens look like regular mittens from the back but open to reveal a short inner cuff that frees your fingers for dexterous tasks. They are constructed just as regular mittens to the base of the fingers, then the palm stitches are placed on hold and new stitches are cast on to replace them. Work continues in the round to the top of the mitten. The held stitches are worked later to create the inner cuff. A classic staghorn cable adorns the back of the hand.

Children's (Women's Medium, Women's Large, Men's)

FINISHED MEASUREMENTS
Approximately 6¾ (7½, 8¼, 9)"
circumference

YARN
Brown Sheep Company Lamb's Pride Worsted (85% wool / 15% mohair; 190 yards [173 meters] / 113 grams): 1 (1, 2, 2) skeins #M22 autumn harvest (#M113 oregano, #M113 oregano, #M06 deep charcoal)

NEEDLES
One set of five double-pointed needles (dpn) size US 6 (4 mm)
One set of five double-pointed needles size US 7 (4.5 mm)
Change needle size if necessary to obtain correct gauge.

NOTIONS
Stitch markers; cable needle (cn); waste yarn in contrasting color; two ½" (13 mm) buttons

GAUGE
20 sts and 28 rnds = 4" (10 cm) in Stockinette stitch (St st) using larger needles

16 sts = 2¼" (5.5 cm) over Staghorn Cable using larger needles

STITCH PATTERNS

Cuff Pattern
(multiple of 4 sts; 6-rnd repeat)
Set-up Rnd: *K3, p1; repeat from * around.
Rnd 1: *K2, k1 wrapping yarn around needle twice, p1; repeat from * around.
Rnd 2: *K2, slip 1 st purlwise wyib dropping extra wrap, p1; repeat from * around.
Rnd 3: *T3R, p1; repeat from * around.
Rnd 4: *K1 wrapping yarn around needle twice, k2, p1; repeat from * around.
Rnd 5: *Slip 1 st purlwise wyib dropping extra wrap, k2, p1; repeat from * around.
Rnd 6: *C3L, p1; repeat from * around.
Repeat Rnds 1-6 for Cuff Pattern.

1x1 Rib
(multiple of 2 sts; 1-rnd repeat)
All Rnds: *K1, p1; repeat from * around.

ABBREVIATIONS
T3R (Twist 3 Right): Knit into front of third st on left-hand needle, knit into front of first st on left-hand needle, dropping it off the needle, then knit into front of next st on left-hand needle, dropping it and the previously-knit third st off at the same time.

C3L (Cross 3 Left): Slip next st to cn and hold to front, k2, k1 from cn.

Right Mitten

CUFF

With Long-Tail CO (see page 136) and smaller needles, CO 32 (36, 40, 44) sts, divide among 4 needles [8-8-8-8 (8-8-8-12, 8-12-8-12, 8-12-12-12)]. Join for working in the rnd, being careful not to twist sts; place marker (pm) for beginning of rnd. Begin Cuff Pattern. Work Set-up Rnd once, work Rnds 1-6 two (three, three, three) times, then work Rnds 1-3 one (zero, zero, one) time.

HAND

Change to larger needles.

Children's Size Only

Increase Rnd: K1, M1L, [k3, M1L] twice, k2, M1L, [k3, M1L] twice, knit to end–38 sts.

Adult Sizes Only

Increase Rnd: K1 (2, 1), [M1L, k3 (3, 4)] 5 times, M1, knit to end–42 (46, 50) sts.

All Sizes

Redistribute sts among 4 needles [11-11-8-8 (12-12-9-9, 13-13-10-10, 14-14-11-11)].

Next rnd: K1 (2, 3, 4), p2, pm, work Staghorn Cable Chart over next 16 sts, pm, p2, knit to end of rnd. *[Note: Needles 1 and 2 hold the sts for the back of the hand, and Needles 3 and 4 hold the sts for the palm and Thumb.]* Work even for 2 rnds.

SHAPE THUMB

Increase Rnd 1: Work 22 (24, 26, 28) sts, pm for Thumb, M1L, k2, M1R, pm, knit to end–40 (44, 48, 52) sts. Work even for 2 rnds.

STAGHORN CABLE CHART

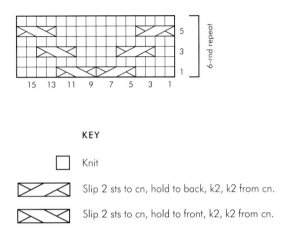

15 13 11 9 7 5 3 1

6-rnd repeat

KEY

☐ Knit

⬛ Slip 2 sts to cn, hold to back, k2, k2 from cn.

⬛ Slip 2 sts to cn, hold to front, k2, k2 from cn.

Increase Rnd 2: Work to first Thumb marker, slip marker (sm), M1L, knit to second Thumb marker, M1R, sm, knit to end–42 (46, 50, 54) sts. Work even for 2 rnds.

Repeat last 3 rnds 1 (3, 3, 4) times, then repeat Increase Rnd 2 once–46 (54, 58, 64) sts.

Next Rnd: Work to first Thumb marker, transfer next 10 (14, 14, 16) sts to waste yarn for Thumb, removing Thumb markers, CO 2 sts over gap, knit to end–38 (42, 46, 50) sts remain. Work even for 3 (4, 4, 6) rnds.

CREATE FLIP-TOP

Work 22 (24, 26, 28) sts, transfer next 16 (18, 20, 22) sts to waste yarn for Inner Palm Cuff, CO 16 (18, 20, 22) sts using Backward Loop CO (see page 136), work to end. *[Note: It is easiest to CO all new sts to one dpn, then divide them between Needles 3 and 4 on the following rnd.]*

Rnds 1 and 2: Continuing in the rnd, work 22 (24, 26, 28) sts, change to 1x1 Rib and work to end.

Children's Size and Women's Size Large Only

Rnd 3 (Buttonhole Rnd): Work 28 (34) sts, ssk, yo, work to end.

Women's Size Medium and Men's Size Only

Rnd 3 (Buttonhole Rnd): Work 33 (39) sts, yo, k2tog, work to end.

All Sizes

Rnds 4 and 5: Repeat Rnd 1.
Rnd 6: Work 22 (24, 26, 28) sts, change to St st and work to end. Work even until piece is long enough to cover fingertips [approximately 5¼ (7, 7½, 8½)" from end of Cuff].

SHAPE TOP

Children's Size Only

Decrease Rnd 1: P2tog, [k2tog] 8 times, p2tog, *k2tog; repeat from * around–19 sts remain.

Adult Sizes Only

Decrease Rnd 1: [K2tog] 1 (1, 2) times, p2tog, [k2tog] 8 times, p2tog, *k2tog; repeat from * around–21 (23, 25) sts remain.

All Sizes

Decrease Rnd 2: *K2tog; repeat from * to last st, k1–10 (11, 12, 13) sts remain. Cut yarn, leaving a 6" tail. Draw through remaining sts, pull tight and fasten off, with tail to the inside.

WORK INNER PALM CUFF

With Long-Tail CO and larger dpn, CO 16 (18, 20, 22) sts, divide sts between 2 needles [8-8 (9-9, 10-10, 11-11)]. Transfer Inner Palm Cuff sts from waste yarn to 2 additional larger dpns. With RS facing, knit across Inner Palm Cuff sts. Join for working in the rnd; pm for beginning of rnd. Begin 1x1 Rib. Work even for 5 rnds. BO all sts in pattern.

THUMB

Transfer Thumb sts from waste yarn to larger dpn. Rejoin yarn; pick up and knit 2 sts from sts CO over gap–12 (16, 16, 18) sts. Join for working in the rnd; pm for beginning of rnd. Work even in St st until piece is long enough to cover thumb [approximately 11 (14, 14, 16) rnds].

Decrease Rnd: *K2tog; repeat from * around–6 (8, 8, 9) sts remain. Cut yarn, leaving a 6" tail. Draw through remaining sts, pull tight and fasten off, with tail to the inside.

Left Mitten

Work as for Right Mitten to beginning of Thumb Shaping.

SHAPE THUMB

Increase Rnd 1: Work 36 (40, 44, 48) sts, pm for Thumb, M1L, k2, M1R–40 (44, 48, 52) sts. Work even for 2 rnds.

Increase Rnd 2: Work to Thumb marker, sm, M1L, knit to end, M1R–42 (46, 50, 54) sts. Work even for 2 rnds.

Repeat last 3 rnds 1 (3, 3, 4) times, then repeat Increase Rnd 2 once–46 (54, 58, 64) sts.

Next Rnd: Work to Thumb marker, transfer next 10 (14, 14, 16) sts to waste yarn for Thumb, removing Thumb marker, CO 2 sts over gap–38 (42, 46, 50) sts remain. Work even for 3 (4, 4, 6) rnds. Complete as for Right Mitten.

FINISHING

Turn Mitten WS out. Arrange Inner Palm Cuff so that it is encircling the Mitten at the same height all around and is not twisted. Sew the lower edge of the Inner Cuff to the back of the Mitten, being careful not to let sts show on RS. Turn Mitten RS out and check fit of Inner Cuff before fastening off sewing strand. Adjust if necessary. Sew button to Inner Cuff to correspond to button-hole. Repeat for second Mitten. Weave in ends.

Negative Space

The interesting construction of this fingerless mitten
is rooted in the shape of a Norwegian-style mitten
called a *brudevott*, or *kirkevott,* worn at weddings or
to church. They are alternatively known as *halvvanter
med tunge,* or half-gloves with a tongue. Having
the palm side open and the back of the hand covered
has its advantages: The hand is partially shielded
from the elements, yet you can still use your fingers
to dig into pockets for keys, take a photo, or even knit
outside in the cold. Stitches are provisionally cast on,
the mitten is worked to the tip, then the provisional
cast-on is undone and an I-cord bind-off is worked,
which continues into an I-cord coil forming the
cuff. The cutaway section of the mitten is also edged
in I-cord, giving it a substantial shape.

△△△△△△△△△

Coiled Icord

Sizes

One size (to fit average woman)

Finished Measurements

Approximately 7½" circumference

Yarn

Reynolds Lopi (100% Icelandic wool;
110 yards [100 meters] / 100 grams):
2 balls #9966 cypress green heather

Needles

One set of five double-pointed needles
(dpn) size US 10 (6 mm)
One set of five double-pointed needles
size US 10½ (6.5 mm)
Change needle size if necessary to obtain
correct gauge.

Notions

Crochet hook size J/10 (6 mm);
stitch marker; safety pin; waste yarn in
contrasting color

Gauge

14 sts and 19 rnds = 4" (10 cm) in
Stockinette stitch (St st) using
smaller needles

Left Glove

With crochet hook and waste yarn, work crochet chain 30 sts long. Fasten off.

With one smaller dpn and working yarn, pick up and knit 26 sts from the "bumps" of the chain. Divide sts among 4 smaller needles [7-6-7-6]. Join for working in the rnd, being careful not to twist sts; place marker (pm) for beginning of rnd. Knit 3 rnds.

Shape Thumb

Place a safety pin in the thirteenth st.

Increase Rnd 1: K12, M1R, k1 (marked st), M1L, knit to end–28 sts. Knit 2 rnds.
Increase Rnd 2: Knit to marked st, M1R, k1, M1L, knit to end–30 sts.
Repeat last 3 rnds twice–34 sts. Knit 1 rnd.
Next Rnd: K12, transfer next 9 sts to waste yarn for Thumb, CO 1 st over gap, knit to end–26 sts remain. Knit 4 rnds.

Shape Cutout

Next Rnd: K2, BO 9 sts, k15–17 sts remain. Knit first 2 sts of the rnd again; place all sts on one dpn.
Next Row (WS): Change to working back and forth. Purl.
Decrease Row: K2, ssk, knit to last 4 sts, k2tog, k2–15 sts remain. Purl 1 row.
Rep Decrease Row every other row 4 times–7 sts remain. Purl 1 row.
Next Row (RS): K2, dcd, k2–5 sts remain. Purl 1 row.
Next Row: K1, dcd, k1–3 sts remain. BO remaining sts.

Thumb

Transfer the 9 sts from waste yarn to 3 smaller dpns. Rejoin yarn; pick up and knit 1 st from st CO over gap–10 sts. Join for working in the rnd; pm for beginning of rnd. Knit 4 rnds. BO all sts.

Right Glove

Work as for Left Glove to beginning of Thumb Shaping.

SHAPE THUMB

Place a safety pin in the first st.

Increase Rnd 1: M1R, k1 (marked st), M1L, knit to end–28 sts. Knit 2 rnds.
Increase Rnd 2: Knit to marked st, M1R, k1, M1L, knit to end–30 sts.
Repeat last 3 rnds twice–34 sts. Knit 1 rnd.
Next Rnd: Transfer next 9 sts to waste yarn for Thumb, CO 1 st over gap, knit to end–26 sts remain. Complete as for Left Glove.

FINISHING

Cuff

Undo crochet chain by pulling out end of chain that was fastened off and unzipping chain, exposing live sts. Transfer sts to 3 larger dpns [8-8-10]. CO 3 sts on fourth dpn and, beginning at side of hand and using fourth and fifth dpns, work I-Cord BO (see page 138) until there are 3 sts left on working dpn. Change to Applied I-Cord (see page 138), working into I-Cord BO just completed to form a coiled Cuff, as follows: pick up and knit 1 st out of the middle of the second st of the I-Cord BO (1½ sts will be showing on the RS), slide sts back to other end of dpn, k2, k2tog-tbl. Continue in this fashion, picking up 1 st from Applied I-Cord when you have worked around I-Cord BO, until you have gone round the entire Cuff 3 more times (you should have 4 coils), working to just past where I-Cord BO began. Cut yarn, leaving a 6" tail. Draw through remaining sts, pull tight and fasten off. Sew end neatly to coil below. Repeat for other Glove.

Cutout Edging

With larger dpns and beginning at BO top of Cutout, work 3-st Applied I-Cord around Cutout edge, ending at BO sts. Cut yarn, leaving a 6" tail. Draw through remaining sts, pull tight and fasten off. Sew end neatly to beginning of I-Cord.

Weave in ends.

PLUSH

The soft, loop-knit cuffs of these mittens cushion the wrists in comfort while the wovenlike stitch pattern on the hand shuffles around the colors of the variegated yarn for a uniform effect (rather than the pooling and stacking effect that often occurs when this type of yarn is worked in many other stitch patterns). Sizes are included for both children and women.

Sizes

Child's (Women's Medium, Women's Large)

Finished Measurements

Approximately 6½ (7½, 8)" circumference

Yarn

Manos del Uruguay Wool (100% wool; 138 yards [126 meters] / 100 grams): 1 (2, 2) hanks #118

Needles

One set of five double-pointed needles (dpn) size US 9 (5.5 mm)
Change needle size if necessary to obtain correct gauge.

Notions

Stitch marker; waste yarn in contrasting color

Gauge

16 sts and 26 rnds = 4" (10 cm) in Half-Linen Stitch

Stitch Pattern

Half-Linen Stitch
(multiple of 2 sts; 4-rnd repeat)
Rnd 1: *K1, slip 1 purlwise wyif; repeat from * around.
Rnds 2 and 4: Knit.
Rnd 3: *Slip 1 purlwise wyif, k1; repeat from * around.
Repeat Rnds 1-4 for Half-Linen Stitch.

Abbreviations

ML (Make Loop): Knit into next st, but do not drop from needle, bring yarn forward between needle tips, wrap once around left thumb, bring yarn to back between needle tips, knit into back of same st, dropping it from left-hand needle, but leaving loop on thumb, insert tip of left-hand needle into fronts of last 2 sts on right-hand needle, k2tog-tbl, drop loop from thumb.

Mittens (both alike)

Cuff

CO 20 (24, 26) sts, divide among 4 needles [5-5-5-5 (6-6-6-6, 6-7-6-7)]. Join for working in the rnd, being careful not to twist sts; place marker (pm) for beginning of rnd.
Rnd 1: Knit.
Rnd 2: *ML; repeat from * around.
Repeat Rnds 1 and 2 three (four, four) times, then repeat Rnd 1 once.

Hand

Increase Rnd: Knit, increase 6 sts evenly spaced around—26 (30, 32) sts.
Next Rnd: Change to Half-Linen Stitch. Work even until piece measures approximately 2 (2½, 2¾)" from Increase Rnd, ending with Rnd 1 or 3 of Half-Linen Stitch.

Thumb Opening

Next Rnd: K14 (16, 17), change to waste yarn and k5 (6, 6), slip these 5 (6, 6) sts back to left-hand needle, change to working yarn, knit these 5 (6, 6) sts again, work to end. Work even until Mitten measures approximately 5¼ (6¾, 7¼)" from Increase Rnd, or until piece is long enough to cover fingertips.

Shape Mitten Top

Next Rnd: *K2tog; repeat from * to end–13 (15, 16) sts remain.
Next Rnd: *K2tog; repeat from * to last 1 (1, 0) st, k1 (1, 0)–7 (8, 8) sts remain. Cut yarn, leaving a 6" tail. Draw through remaining sts, pull tight and fasten off, with tail to the inside.

Thumb

Carefully remove waste yarn from Thumb sts and place bottom 5 (6, 6) sts and top 6 (7, 7) sts onto 2 dpns. Rejoin working yarn, pick up and knit 2 sts at side of Thumb Opening, knit across 5 (6, 6) bottom sts, pick up and knit 2 sts at other side of Thumb Opening, knit across 4 (5, 5) top sts, k2tog–14 (16, 16) sts. Distribute sts among 3 needles. Join for working in the rnd; pm for beginning of rnd.

Next Rnd: Slip 1, k2tog, k3 (4, 4), ssk, k2tog, k3 (4, 4), ssk (last st of rnd and first st of next rnd)–10 (12, 12) sts remain. Begin Half-Linen Stitch, aligning with palm stitches. Work even until piece is long enough to cover Thumb.
Next Rnd: *K2tog; repeat from * around–5 (6, 6) sts remain. Cut yarn, leaving a 6" tail. Draw through remaining sts, pull tight and fasten off, with tail to the inside.

Weave in ends.

POPPY

The mohair ruffles of these gloves are
knit first in rows, then worked with the cuff
stitches later. I think the ruffles resemble
the delicate petals of a poppy after they have
emerged from the bud. Block the ruffles
when you have finished knitting to prevent
them from curling up.

ruffles

Women's Small (Medium, Large)

FINISHED MEASUREMENTS
Approximately 7¼ (7½, 8)" circumference

YARN
Naturally Alpine DK/8-ply (100% pure New Zealand wool; 437 yards [400 meters] / 200 grams): 1 hank #1002 pale green (MC)

Naturally Mist 1-ply (80% superfine kid mohair / 20% nylon; 181 yards [166 meters] / 25 grams): 1 ball #605 chartreuse (A)

NEEDLES
One pair straight needles size US 4 (3.5 mm)
One set of five double-pointed needles (dpn) size US 4 (3.5 mm)
Change needle size if necessary to obtain correct gauge.

NOTIONS
Stitch markers; waste yarn in contrasting color; tapestry needle

GAUGE
23 sts and 29 rnds = 4" (10 cm) in Stockinette stitch (St st) using MC

RUFFLES (MAKE 10)
With straight needles, Long-Tail CO (see page 136), and A, CO 60 (63, 66) sts, leaving a long tail. Begin St st; work even for 3 rows, beginning with a purl row.
Decrease Row: *K1, k2tog; repeat from * to end—40 (42, 44) sts remain. Cut yarn; transfer sts to waste yarn.

Left Glove

CUFF
With dpns, Long-Tail CO, and MC, CO 40 (42, 44) sts, divide among 4 dpns [10-10-10-10 (11-10-11-10, 11-11-11-11)]. Join for working in the rnd, being careful not to twist sts; place marker (pm) for beginning of rnd. Knit 1 rnd. *[Note: Needles 1 and 2 hold the sts for the palm, and Needles 3 and 4 hold the sts for the back of the hand.]*

Next Rnd (Join Ruffle): Holding Ruffle at RS of Glove, with RS of Ruffle facing out, *slip first st of Ruffle to left-hand needle, k2tog (first st on left-hand needle with first st of Ruffle); repeat from * to end. *[Note: Leave Ruffle sts on waste yarn until rnd is complete, then remove waste yarn.]* Work even in St st for 3 rnds. Repeat last 4 rnds 4 times.

HAND
Increase Rnd: *K20 (21, 22), M1R; repeat from * to end—42 (44, 46) sts. Work even until piece measures approximately 2½ (2¾, 2¾)" from last increase rnd.

THUMB OPENING
Next Rnd: K12 (13, 14), change to waste yarn and k8, slip these 8 sts back to left-hand needle, change to working yarn, knit these 8 sts again, work to end. Work even until piece reaches base of fingers [approximately 10 (11, 12) more rnds].

DIVIDE FOR FINGERS
Transfer all sts from Needle 2 to Needle 1 for palm of hand, and all sts from Needle 4 to Needle 3 for back of hand—21 (22, 23) sts on each needle.

[Note: Use a piece of waste yarn threaded on a tapestry needle to hold the sts for each Finger.]

Pinkie: Transfer first 5 sts from Needle 1 and last 5 sts from Needle 3 to waste yarn—10 sts. **Ring Finger:** Transfer next 4 (5, 5) sts from each of Needles 1 and 3 to waste yarn—8 (10, 10) sts. **Middle Finger:** Transfer next 5 (5, 6) sts from each of Needles 1 and 3 to waste yarn—10 (10, 12) sts. **Index Finger:** Transfer remaining 7 sts from each of Needles 1 and 3 to waste yarn—14 sts.

PINKIE
Transfer sts from waste yarn to dpns. K5 (palm sts), CO 2 sts over gap between Pinkie and Ring Finger, k5 (back of hand sts)—12 sts. Join for working in the rnd; pm for beginning of rnd. Work in St st until piece is long enough to cover Pinkie (approximately 17 rnds).

Decrease Rnd: *K2tog; repeat from * to end—6 sts remain. Cut yarn, leaving a 6" tail. Draw through remaining sts, pull tight and fasten off, with tail to the inside.

RING FINGER AND MIDDLE FINGER

Working one Finger at a time, transfer sts from waste yarn to dpns. Rejoin MC; pick up and knit 2 sts from sts CO between previous Finger and current Finger, k4 (5, 5) for Ring Finger [k5 (5, 6) for Middle Finger], CO 2 sts over gap between current Finger and next Finger, k4 (5, 5) for Ring Finger [k5 (5, 6) for Middle Finger]–12 (14, 14) sts for Ring Finger [14 (14, 16) sts for Middle Finger]. Join for working in the rnd; pm for beginning of rnd. Work in St st until piece is long enough to cover finger (approximately 22 rnds for Ring Finger; 24 rnds for Middle Finger). Complete as for Pinkie–6 (7, 7) sts remain for Ring Finger [7, (7, 8) sts for Middle Finger].

INDEX FINGER

Transfer sts from waste yarn to dpns. Rejoin MC; pick up and knit 2 sts from sts CO between Middle Finger and Index Finger, k14–16 sts. Join for working in the rnd; pm for beginning of rnd. Work in St st until piece is long enough to cover Index Finger (approximately 22 rnds). Complete as for Pinkie–8 sts remain.

THUMB

Carefully remove waste yarn from Thumb sts and place bottom 8 sts and top 9 sts onto 2 dpns, being careful not to twist sts. Rejoin MC; pick up and knit 2 sts at side of Thumb Opening, knit across 8 bottom sts, pick up and knit 2 sts at other side of Thumb Opening, knit across 9 top sts–21 sts. Distribute sts evenly among 3 dpns. Join for working in the rnd; pm for beginning of rnd.

Next Rnd: K1, k2tog, k6, ssk, k2tog, k7, ssk (last st of rnd together with first st of next rnd)–17 sts remain. Work even in St st until piece is long enough to cover Thumb (approximately 21 rnds). **Decrease Rnd:** *K2tog; repeat from * to last st, k1–9 sts remain. Cut yarn, leaving a 6" tail. Draw through remaining sts, pull tight and fasten off, with tail to the inside.

Right Glove

Work as for Left Glove to Thumb Opening. [Note: Terms for "back of hand" and "palm" should be reversed.]

THUMB OPENING

Next Rnd: K22 (23, 24), change to waste yarn and k8, slip these 8 sts back to left-hand needle, change to working yarn, knit these 8 sts again, work to end. Complete as for Left Glove, working Fingers in the same order.

FINISHING

Sew side edges of Ruffles together, using CO tails. Block Gloves, pinning Ruffles down and steaming with iron and damp cloth in order to make them lie flat. Weave in ends.

RUSALKA

These fingerless gloves are worked in a yarn
made of silk and SeaCell, a new fiber derived
from seaweed. Sea minerals are absorbed
by the skin as you knit and wear this yarn—what
an unusual way to get your vitamins! The beads
are sewn on with gold thread after knitting;
the purled pattern in the cuff serves as an easy
guide for adding the beads. I chose gold
thread for beading because, wherever it shows,
it shines like sunlight on the sea. Rusalka is
the name of a Slavic water-dwelling fairy creature.

finger bridges

Women's Small/Medium (Large)

FINISHED MEASUREMENTS
Approximately 6¾ (7¼)" circumference.
Note: Silk will stretch when worn.

YARN
Hand Maiden Sea Silk (70% silk /
30% SeaCell; 437 yards [400 meters] /
100 grams): 1 hank Nova Scotia

NEEDLES
One set of five double-pointed needles
(dpn) size US 2½ (3 mm)
Change needle size if necessary to
obtain correct gauge.

NOTIONS
Stitch marker; removable markers; 6 mm
bugle beads in coordinating color;
beading needle with eye small enough
to pass through beads; 8 yards gold
metallic thread

GAUGE
28 sts and 36 rows = 4" (10 cm) in
Stockinette stitch (St st)

Left Glove

With Long-Tail CO (see page 136), CO 48 sts,
divide evenly among 4 needles. Join for working in
the rnd, being careful not to twist sts; place marker
(pm) for beginning of rnd. *[Note: Needles 1 and
2 hold the sts for the palm and Thumb, and Needles
3 and 4 hold the sts for the back of the hand.]* Begin
St st. Work even for 2 rnds.

Next Rnd: Begin Cuff Chart. Work even for 18
rnds.
Next Rnd: Change to St st. Work even for 2 rnds.
Eyelet Rnd: *K2, yo, k2tog; repeat from * to end.

SIZE LARGE ONLY
Increase Rnd: *K24, M1L; repeat from * to end–50 sts.

BOTH SIZES
Work even for 8 rnds.

SHAPE THUMB
Increase Rnd 1: K23 (24), pm, M1R, k2, M1L, pm,
knit to end–50 (52) sts. Work even for 2 rnds.
Increase Rnd 2: Knit to first marker, slip marker (sm),
M1R, knit to next marker, M1L, sm, knit to end–52
(54) sts.
Repeat last 3 rnds 5 times–62 (64) sts. Work even
for 1 rnd.
Next Rnd: K23 (24), transfer next 16 sts to waste yarn
for Thumb, CO 2 sts over gap, knit to end–48 (50) sts
remain. Work even until piece is long enough to reach
base of fingers.

SHAPE FINGER SPACES
Next Rnd: BO 24 (25) sts, placing removable markers
between BO sts as follows: First marker 5 sts from
beg of rnd, second marker 6 sts after first marker, third
marker 6 (7) sts after second marker (7 sts remain to
end of BO). BO next 7 sts, *[yo, pass last knit st over yo
and off right-hand needle] 4 (5) times, insert right-hand
needle into space where third marker is, pick up and
knit 1 st, then pass next-to-last st over picked-up
st and off right-hand needle. Working back along short
yo chain, pick up 1 st in each loop of chain, then pass
next-to-last st over picked-up st and off right-hand
needle, until you reach left-hand needle again.* BO next
6 (7) sts, then repeat from * to *. BO next 6 sts, then
repeat from * to *. *[Note: You are creating small bridges
to the other side of the Glove.]* BO remaining 5 sts.

THUMB
Transfer sts from waste yarn to dpns. Rejoin yarn; pick
up and knit 2 sts from sts CO over gap–18 sts. Knit 4
rnds. BO all sts.

Right Glove

Work as for Left Glove, working Finger Spaces in the same order. *[Note: Terms for "back of hand" and "palm" should be reversed.]*

FINISHING

Block Gloves lightly.

Twisted Cords (make 2)

Cut 3 strands of yarn approximately 60" long. With all 3 strands held together, tie one end to a stationary object. Twist strands until Cord begins to double up on itself tightly. Distribute twist evenly, tie ends together with overhand knot and trim. Tie overhand knot in folded end and trim. Thread Cord through eyelet rnd and tie at side of hand. Trim again if desired.

Beads

With gold thread threaded on a beading needle, sew bugle beads to patterned section of cuff, using the purl sts as a guideline, and sewing beads alongside purl sts (see photo), as follows: Knot thread and secure on WS, at the point where you wish to begin. Bring needle through to RS, thread bead onto needle, pull needle and thread through bead, pass needle to WS at very end of bead. *Bring needle through to RS at beg of last bead, insert needle through bead again, and thread another bead onto needle, pull needle and thread through bead, pass needle to WS at very end of bead. Repeat from * until bead motif is complete. For more information, see page 135.

CUFF CHART

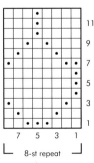

7 5 3 1

8-st repeat

KEY

☐ Knit

⊡ Purl

SHELTIE

The soft mohair underlayer blooms through the
openwork overlay of these dual-layered mittens.
Air is trapped between the layers and warmed
by your hands, providing insulation. The overlay
is worked in an old Shetland pattern called
Bird's Eye (collected by Barbara G. Walker in
A Treasury of Knitting Patterns). The name "Sheltie"
is an Anglicization of the Gaelic *sealtaí*, meaning
Shetland pony. Shetland ponies grow dual
coats for the winter that insulate them against the
wind and weather as they forage for seaweed
along the shore.

layered knitting stitch

SIZES

One size (to fit average woman)

FINISHED MEASUREMENTS

Approximately 8" Underlayer circumference

YARN

Garnstudio Vienna (90% mohair / 10% polyester; 104 yards [95 meters] / 50 grams): 1 ball #21 winter white (MC)

Garnstudio Alaska (100% wool; 82 yards [75 meters] / 50 grams): 2 balls #50 brown heather (A)

NEEDLES

One set of five double-pointed needles (dpn) size US 9 (5.5 mm)

One pair straight needles size US 9 (5.5 mm)

Change needle size if necessary to obtain correct gauge.

NOTIONS

Stitch marker; removable st marker; waste yarn in contrasting color

GAUGE

13 sts and 19 rnds = 4" (10 cm) in Stockinette stitch (St st) using MC

14 sts and 20 rows = 4" (10 cm) in Bird's Eye Pattern using A

NOTE

This Mitten consists of two parts: a mohair Underlayer and a wool Overlay in an openwork pattern, which allows the mohair to be seen. The Underlayer is worked in the round. The Overlay is worked flat, then sewn up.

STITCH PATTERN

Bird's Eye Pattern
(multiple of 4 sts; 4-row repeat)

Row 1 (WS): *K2tog, [yo] twice, k2tog; repeat from * to end.

Row 2: *K1, [k1, p1] into double yo, k1; repeat from * to end.

Row 3: K2, *k2tog, [yo] twice, k2tog; repeat from * to last 2 sts, k2.

Row 4: K2, *k1, [k1, p1] into double yo, k1; repeat from * to last 2 sts, k2.

Repeat Rows 1-4 for Bird's Eye Pattern.

Underlayer (both mittens alike)

With MC, Long-Tail CO (see page 136), and dpns, CO 26 sts, divide among 4 needles [7-6-7-6]. Join for working in the rnd, being careful not to twist sts; place marker (pm) for beginning of rnd. Begin St st; work even for 25 rnds (piece should measure approximately 5¼" from the beginning).

THUMB OPENING

Next Rnd: K14, change to waste yarn and k5, slip these 5 sts back to left-hand needle, change to MC, knit these 5 sts again, work to end. Work even until piece is long enough to cover fingers (approximately 20 rows; piece should measure approximately 9¾" from the beginning).

Decrease Rnd 1: *K2tog; repeat from * to end–13 sts remain.

Decrease Rnd 2: *K2tog; repeat from * to last st, k1–7 sts remain. Cut yarn, leaving a 6" tail. Draw through remaining sts, pull tight and fasten off, with tail to the inside.

THUMB

Carefully remove waste yarn from Thumb sts and place bottom 5 sts and top 6 sts onto 2 dpns. Rejoin MC; pick up and knit 1 st at side of Thumb Opening, knit across 5 bottom sts, pick up and knit 1 st at other side of Thumb Opening, knit across 6 top sts–13 sts. Distribute sts among 3 dpns. Join for working in the rnd; pm for beginning of rnd.

Rnd 1: K2tog, k3, ssk, k6–11 sts remain. Work even until piece is long enough to cover thumb (approximately 12 rnds).

Decrease Rnd: *K2tog; repeat from * to last st, k1–6 sts remain. Cut yarn, leaving a 6" tail. Draw through remaining sts, pull tight and fasten off, with tail to the inside.

Overlay

RIGHT OVERLAY

With straight needles, Long-Tail CO and A, CO 28 sts. Begin Bird's Eye Pattern. Work even for 18 rows (piece should measure approximately 3¾" from the beginning). Place a marker on the RS of the work.

Thumb Opening

Next Row (WS): K2, k2tog, [yo] twice, k2tog, k2, transfer next 5 sts to waste yarn for Thumb, CO 5 sts over gap using Backward Loop CO (see page 136), k1, *k2tog, [yo] twice, k2tog; repeat from * to last 2 sts, k2.

Next Row: Continue in pattern, knitting the 5 CO sts. Work even, working pattern over entire row, until piece measures approximately 8½" from the beginning, ending with a RS row.

Decrease Row (WS): *K2tog; repeat from * to end–14 sts remain. Repeat Decrease Row once–7 sts remain. Cut yarn, leaving a very long tail. Draw through remaining sts, pull tight and fasten off. Using tail, sew side seam, making sure RS is on the outside.

Thumb

[*Note: Thumb is worked flat, but it will be easier to work with 2 dpns, rather than straight needles.*]

With RS of Overlay facing, and with CO edge facing away from you (Mitten is upside-down), carefully remove waste yarn from Thumb sts, and transfer sts to dpn, being careful not to twist sts, then using Long-Tail CO and A, CO 7 sts at end of row (your left)–12 sts. Cut yarn and slide sts to opposite end of dpn. Do NOT turn work. Rejoin A, ready to work a WS row.

Next Row (WS): Begin Bird's Eye Pattern, beginning with Row 3. Work even for 14 rows.

Decrease Row: *K2tog; repeat from * to end–6 sts remain. Cut yarn, leaving a 12" tail. Draw through remaining sts, pull tight and fasten off. Using tail, sew Thumb seam. Sew bottom of Thumb neatly to sts CO over Thumb Opening.

LEFT OVERLAY

Work as for Right Overlay to beginning of Thumb Opening.

Thumb Opening

Next Row (WS): K2, [k2tog, [yo] twice, k2tog] 3 times, k1, transfer next 5 sts to waste yarn for Thumb, CO 5 sts over gap using Backward Loop CO, k2, k2tog, [yo] twice, k2tog, k2.

Next Row: Continue in pattern, knitting the 5 CO sts. Work as for Right Overlay to beginning of Thumb.

Thumb

With RS of Overlay facing, and with CO edge facing toward you (Mitten is right-side-up), carefully remove waste yarn from Thumb sts and transfer sts to dpn, being careful not to twist sts. Using Long-Tail CO and A, CO 7 sts at end of row (your left)–12 sts. Do NOT cut yarn. Turn work, ready to work a WS row across CO sts first, then held sts. Complete as for Right Overlay.

FINISHING

Place Underlayers inside Overlays. Allow CO edge of Underlayer to roll up to CO edge of Overlay, and sew in place. If desired, using A, sew both pieces together on the WS at the tip of the hand and the Thumb.

Snug

I first encountered ultra-warm thrummed mittens, worked with a combination of yarn and short pieces of roving (called thrums), a few years ago in a gift shop in Toronto. The mittens in the shop were made in Newfoundland, where the winters are harsh and snowy. I spent the first eighteen years of my life in a similar climate (in Cape Breton) but, oddly enough, had never seen a pair of these mittens. To add to the insulating qualities of my thrummed mittens, I designed a snug wind- and snow-proof cuff by folding a length of ribbing to the inside and stitching it down after knitting. The outside of the cuff features rings of reverse Stockinette stitch, which lend an air of sculptural grace.

SIZE
Child's (Woman's)

FINISHED MEASUREMENTS
Approximately 7 (8)" circumference

YARN
Fleece Artist Blue Face Leicester Aran (100% wool; 410 yards [375 meters] / 250 grams): 1 hank bronze (MC)

Fleece Artist Blue Face Leicester Sliver Roving (100% wool; 50 grams): 1 braid lichen (A)

NEEDLES
One set of five double-pointed needles (dpn) size US 7 (4.5 mm)
Change needle size if necessary to obtain correct gauge.

NOTIONS
Stitch markers; waste yarn in contrasting color

GAUGE
18 sts and 24 rnds = 4" (10 cm) in Stockinette stitch (St st)

NOTE
The thrums are created by taking short pieces of roving and knitting them in as you work. They appear as big puffy stitches on the outside, and fleecy ends on the inside. To prepare roving for making thrums, divide the roving into strips 2 to 3 times the width of MC yarn, then pull off 4" lengths to knit as thrums. When you want to place a thrum, twist it a bit at the middle section, then fold it in half. Insert the right-hand needle into the next st, loop the folded thrum over the needle as you would to wrap a st when knitting and draw the thrum through the st and off the left-hand needle. Run the working yarn behind the stitch, ready to knit the following st. Make Thumb thrums a bit smaller so there will be room for your thumb.

Left Mitten

RIBBED INNER CUFF
With Long-Tail CO (see page 136), CO 28 (32) sts, divide among 4 needles [7-7-7-7 (8-8-8-8)]. Join for working in the rnd, being careful not to twist sts; place marker (pm) for beginning of rnd.
Next Rnd: *K1, p1; repeat from * to end. Work even for 11 (14) rnds.

CUFF
Purl 4 (5) rnds. *Knit 3 (4) rnds. Purl 3 (4) rnds. Repeat from * once.

HAND
Rnd 1: Knit.
Rnd 2: *K1, M1R, k12 (14), M1L, k1; repeat from * to end–32 (36) sts.
Rnds 3 and 4: Knit.
Rnd 5 (Thrum Rnd): *K3, thrum 1; repeat from * to end.

SHAPE THUMB
Rnd 6: K15 (17), pm for Thumb, M1L, knit to end–33 (37) sts.
Rnd 7: Knit to Thumb marker, slip marker (sm), M1L, knit to end–34 (38) sts.
Rnd 8: Knit.
Rnds 9 and 10: Repeat Rnd 7–36 (40) sts after Rnd 10.
Rnd 11 (Thrum Rnd): K1, *thrum 1, k3; repeat from * to last 3 sts, thrum 1, k2.
Rnds 12 and 13: Repeat Rnd 7–38 (42) sts after Rnd 13.
Rnd 14: Knit.
Rnds 15 and 16: Repeat Rnd 7–40 (44) sts after Rnd 16.
Rnd 17: Repeat Rnd 5.

Child's Size Only
Rnd 18: Knit.

Woman's Size Only
Rnds 18 and 19: Repeat Rnd 7–46 sts after Rnd 19.
Rnd 20: Knit.

Rnd 19 (21): K15 (17), transfer next 10 (12) sts to waste yarn for Thumb, CO 2 sts over gap, knit to end–32 (36) sts.
Rnd 20 (22): Knit.

Child's Size Only
Rnds 21 and 22: Knit.

Both Sizes
Rnd 23: Repeat Rnd 11.
Rnds 24-28: Knit.
Rnd 29: Repeat Rnd 5.
Rnds 30-34: Knit.
Rnd 35: Repeat Rnd 11.

Woman's Size Only
Rnds 36-40: Knit.
Rnd 41: Repeat Rnd 5.

MITTEN TOP
Both Sizes
Rnd 36 (42) and alternate rnds: Knit.
Rnd 37 (43): *K2, k2tog; repeat from * to end–24 (27) sts remain.
Rnd 39 (45): *K1, k2tog; repeat from * to end–16 (18) sts remain.
Rnd 41 (47): *K2tog; repeat from * to end–8 (9) sts remain. Cut yarn, leaving a 6" tail. Draw through remaining sts, pull tight and fasten off.

THUMB
Transfer sts from waste yarn to dpns. Rejoin yarn; pick up and knit 2 sts from sts CO over gap–12 (14) sts. Join for working in the rnd; pm for beginning of rnd. Knit 4 (2) rnds.

Thrum Rnd: Work thrums so that they are staggered in relation to last Thrum Rnd worked on Thumb. *[Note: For Woman's Size, since the number of sts is not divisible by 4, you must leave only 2 sts between thrums twice, instead of 3. Do this on inside of Thumb to be less noticeable.]*

Continuing in St st, work even for 5 rnds. Repeat Thrum Rnd, staggering sts in relation to last Thrum Rnd worked. Work even until piece is long enough to cover Thumb.

Decrease Rnd: *K2tog; repeat from * to end–6 (7) sts remain. Cut yarn, leaving a 6" tail. Draw through remaining sts, pull tight and fasten off.

Right Mitten
Work as for Left Mitten to beginning of Thumb Shaping.

SHAPE THUMB
Rnd 6: K17 (19), M1R, pm for Thumb, knit to end–33 (37) sts.
Rnd 7: Knit to Thumb marker, M1R, sm, knit to end–34 (38) sts. Complete as for Left Mitten.

FINISHING
Turn Mitten inside out. Fold Ribbed Inner Cuff to WS and slipstitch neatly to base of hand, being careful not to let sts show on RS. Weave in ends.

Standard Deviation

While watching the 1980 film *The Shining*, one of the images I found striking was the ominous repetition of patterns in the carpeting of the Overlook Hotel. I love the colors and the highly stylized motifs and how variations in color and patterning occur from room to room but are united by a recurring theme. These fingerless gloves are worked in the round in a fine Norwegian wool, from the top edge down, with stitches cast on for the thumb gore and then decreased to the wrist. The main pattern is repeated at the wrist in a deviation from the original color sequence, and the thumb gore features a motif from the main pattern, worked in the negative of the original color sequence. This project is named for a term used in statistical mathematics to describe how far the individual elements vary from the mean.

SIZES

One size (to fit average woman)

FINISHED MEASUREMENTS

Approximately 7¼" circumference

YARN

Rauma Finullgarn (100% wool; 180 yards
[165 meters] / 50 grams): 1 ball each
#410 dark brown (MC), #499 burgundy
(A), #439 fuchsia (B), #445 bright salmon
(C), and #4197 gold (D)

NEEDLES

One set of five double-pointed needles
(dpn) size US 2½ (3 mm)
Change needle size if necessary to obtain
correct gauge.

NOTIONS

Stitch markers; tapestry needle

GAUGE

30 sts and 30 rows = 4" (10 cm) in
Stockinette stitch (St st) over Hand Chart

NOTE

Gloves are worked in the round from
upper edge to lower edge, with extra sts
cast on for the Thumb Gore, which are
then decreased to wrist.

Fingerless Gloves (both alike)

With Long-Tail CO (see page 136) and MC, CO 54 sts,
divide among 4 needles [14-13-14-13]. Join for working
in the rnd, being careful not to twist sts; place marker
(pm) for beginning of rnd.

BEGIN CHART

Rnd 1: Work Hand Chart across 54 sts, carrying colors
not in use loosely up the WS at beginning of Chart.
Work even until entire Rnd 16 is complete.

Rnd 17: Work 26 sts, BO 2 sts, work to end–52 sts remain.

Rnd 18: Work to BO sts, pm, with MC and Backward
Loop CO (see page 136), CO 19 sts for Thumb
Gore (dividing CO sts between Needles 2 and 3), pm,
work to end–71 sts. *[Note: Carry the contrasting color
tightly behind the BO sts; the strand will be worked
into the Thumb Gore finishing.]*

Rnd 19: Work to marker, work across Thumb Gore
Chart, work to end. Work even, working decreases as
shown in Thumb Gore Chart, until Thumb Gore Chart
is complete, removing Thumb Gore markers on last
rnd–54 sts remain.

Rnd 38-44: Work even until Hand Chart is complete.
With MC, BO all sts.

FINISHING

Block Gloves. With MC threaded on tapestry needle,
work Closed Blanket Stitch (see page 136) along sts
BO and CO for Thumb Gore.

KEY

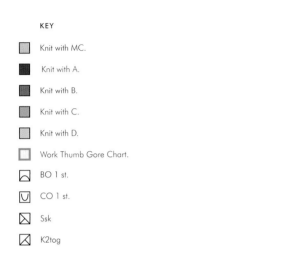

- Knit with MC.
- Knit with A.
- Knit with B.
- Knit with C.
- Knit with D.
- Work Thumb Gore Chart.
- ◿ BO 1 st.
- ◡ CO 1 st.
- ◹ Ssk
- ◿ K2tog

THUMB GORE CHART

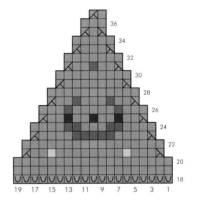

HAND CHART

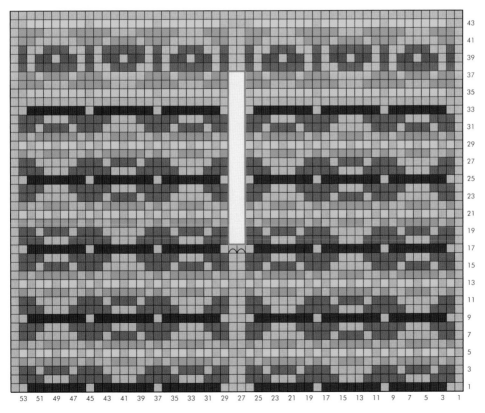

STRATA

I enjoy layering gloves for both warmth and aesthetic purposes, so for this project I created three different layers—Traditional Gloves (with fingers), Short-Fingered Gloves, and Fingerless Gloves—each of which can be worn alone or in combination with one or both of the other layers. The Traditional Gloves and Short-Fingered Gloves are worked in a sport-weight alpaca and silk blend yarn that is fine enough for layering without unnecessary bulk; the Fingerless Gloves are worked in a brushed alpaca that is lofty, not heavy. I hope you'll make several pairs in your favorite colors and mix and match with abandon.

OₒOₒOₒOₒOₒOₒOₒOₒOₒOₒOₒOₒOₒOₒOₒOₒ

SIZES

Traditional Gloves and Short-Fingered
Gloves: Women's Medium (Large, X-Large)
Fingerless Gloves: Women's Medium
(Large)

FINISHED MEASUREMENTS

Traditional Gloves and Short-Fingered
Gloves: Approximately 7½ (8, 8½)"
circumference. Fingerless Gloves:
Approximately 7½ (8)" circumference

YARN

Blue Sky Alpacas Alpaca Silk (50% alpaca
/ 50% silk; 146 yards [133 meters] /
50 grams): Traditional Gloves: 2 hanks
#126 brick, or #137 sapphire (MC);
Short-Fingered Gloves: 1 (2, 2) hanks
#100 slate (A)

Blue Sky Alpacas Brushed Suri (67% baby
suri / 22% merino / 11% bamboo; 142
yards [130 meters] / 50 grams): Fingerless
Gloves: 1 hank #900 whipped cream (B)

NEEDLES

One set of five double-pointed needles
(dpn) size US 3 (3.25 mm)
One set of five double-pointed needles
size US 6 (4 mm)
Change needle size if necessary to obtain
correct gauge.

NOTIONS

Stitch markers; waste yarn in contrasting
color; tapestry needle

GAUGE

26 sts and 34 rnds = 4" (10 cm) in
Stockinette stitch (St st) using smaller
needles and MC or A

20 sts and 28 rnds = 4" (10 cm) in
Stockinette stitch using larger needles
and B

NOTE

When making the Short-Fingered Gloves, make them one
size larger than you made the Gloves if you plan to layer
them over the Gloves. Make them your regular size if you
plan to wear them mainly by themselves or underneath
the Fingerless Gloves. Note that the pattern for the
Traditional Gloves and Short-Fingered Gloves includes
Medium (Large, X-Large) sizing. The Fingerless Gloves
have more give and will fit over the other layers, and
should therefore be made in your regular size.

Use the Backward Loop CO (see page 136) to add sts
over the Thumb gap and between Fingers.

STITCH PATTERN

1x1 Rib
(multiple of 2 sts; 1-rnd repeat)
All Rnds: *K1, p1; repeat from * around.

Traditional Gloves and Short-Fingered Gloves

LEFT GLOVE/SHORT-FINGERED GLOVE

With Long-Tail CO (see page 136), smaller dpn and
MC or A, CO 48 (52, 56) sts, divide evenly among
4 needles [12-12-12-12 (13-13-13-13, 14-14-14-14)].
Join for working in the rnd, being careful not to twist
sts; place marker (pm) for beginning of rnd. *[Note:
Needles 1 and 2 hold the sts for the palm and Thumb,
and Needles 3 and 4 hold the sts for the back of the
hand.]* Begin St st. Work even for 9 rnds.

Decrease Rnd 1: *K10 (11, 12), k2tog; repeat from *
around–44 (48, 52) sts remain. Work even for 9 rnds.
Decrease Rnd 2: *K9 (10, 11), k2tog; repeat from *
around–40 (44, 48) sts remain. Work even for 9 rnds.
Increase Rnd 1: *K10 (11, 12), M1L; repeat from *
around–44 (48, 52) sts remain. Work even for 2 rnds.
Increase Rnd 2: K5 (6, 6), *M1L, k11 (12, 13); repeat
from * to last 6 (6, 7) sts, M1L, knit to end–48 (52, 56)
sts. Work even for 2 rnds.

Shape Thumb

Increase Rnd 3: K22 (24, 26), pm for Thumb, M1L, k2, M1R, pm, knit to end–50 (54, 58) sts. Work even for 2 rnds.

Increase Rnd 4: Knit to first marker, slip marker (sm), M1L, knit to second marker, M1R, sm, knit to end–52 (56, 60) sts. Work even for 2 rnds. Repeat last 3 rnds 4 times, then repeat Increase Rnd 4 once–62 (66, 70) sts. Work even for 1 rnd.

Next Rnd: Knit to first marker, transfer next 16 sts to waste yarn for Thumb, removing Thumb markers, CO 2 sts over gap, knit to end–48 (52, 56) sts remain. Work even until piece is long enough to reach base of Pinkie [approximately 8 (9, 10) rnds], ending 6 (6, 7) sts before end of rnd.

Divide for Fingers

[Note: Use a piece of waste yarn threaded on a tapestry needle to hold the sts for each finger.]
Pinkie: Transfer next 12 (12, 14) sts [last 6 (6, 7) sts of rnd and first 6 (6, 7) of next rnd] to waste yarn, pm, CO 2 sts over gap, knit to 5 (6, 6) sts before marker. **Ring Finger:** Transfer next 12 (14, 14) sts [5 (6, 6) sts from back, 2 CO sts from previous rnd, and 5 (6, 6) sts from palm] to waste yarn, removing marker, pm, CO 2 sts over gap, knit to 6 (6, 7) sts before marker. **Middle Finger:** Transfer next 14 (14, 16) sts [(6 (6, 7) sts from back, 2 CO sts from previous rnd, and 6 (6, 7) sts from palm] to waste yarn, removing marker, pm, CO 2 sts over gap–16 (18, 18) sts remain for Index Finger.

Index Finger

Short-fingered Gloves: Work in St st for 8 rnds. BO all sts.

Gloves: Work in St st until piece is long enough to cover index finger (approximately 24 rnds).
Decrease Rnd: *K2tog; repeat from * around–8 (9, 9) sts remain. Cut yarn, leaving a 6" tail. Draw through remaining sts, pull tight and fasten off, with tail to the inside.

Middle, Ring and Pinkie Fingers, and Thumb

Working one Finger at a time, transfer sts from waste yarn to dpns. Rejoin MC or A; pick up and knit 2 sts from CO between previous Finger and current Finger (or from sts CO over gap for Thumb)–16 (16, 18) sts for Middle Finger [14 (16, 16) sts for Ring Finger; 14 (14, 16) sts for Pinkie; 18 sts for Thumb]. Join for working in the rnd; pm for beginning of rnd.
Short Fingered Gloves: Work in St st for 8 rnds (Middle Finger, Thumb) or 7 rnds (Ring Finger, Pinkie). BO all sts.

Gloves: Work in St st until piece is long enough to cover finger (approximately 26 rnds for Middle Finger, 25 rnds for Ring Finger, 21 rnds for Pinkie, and 21 rnds for Thumb). Complete as for Index Finger–8 (8, 9) sts remain for Middle Finger [7 (8, 8) sts for Ring Finger; 7 (7, 8) sts for Pinkie; 9 sts for Thumb].

Right Glove/Short-Fingered Glove

Work as for Left Glove/Short-Fingered Glove to beginning of Thumb Shaping. *[Note: Terms for "back of hand" and "palm" should be reversed, and Thumb sts will be on Needle 3.]*

Shape Thumb

Increase Rnd 3: K24 (26, 28), pm, M1L, k2, M1R, pm, knit to end–50 (54, 58) sts. Work even for 2 rnds. Complete as for Left Glove/Short-Fingered Glove, working fingers in same order.

Finishing

Weave in ends, using yarn tails from rejoined yarn to close any gaps around the bases of the Fingers and Thumb. Block Gloves/Short-Fingered Gloves.

Fingerless Gloves (both alike)

With Long-Tail CO, larger dpn and B, CO 36 (38) sts, divide among 4 needles [9-9-9-9 (10-9-10-9)]. Join for working in the rnd, being careful not to twist sts; pm for beginning of rnd. Begin 1x1 Rib. Work even for 3 rnds.

Next Rnd: Change to St st. Work even for 3 rnds.
Decrease Rnd 1: *K16 (17), k2tog; repeat from * around–34 (36) sts remain. Work even for 4 rnds.
Decrease Rnd 2: *K15 (16), k2tog; repeat from * around–32 (34) sts remain. Work even for 7 rnds.
Increase Rnd 1: *K16 (17), M1L; repeat from * around–34 (36) sts. Work even for 4 rnds.
Increase Rnd 2: *K8 (9), M1L, k9, M1L; repeat from * around–38 (40) sts. Work even for 2 rnds.

Shape Thumb

Increase Rnd 3: K18 (19), pm, M1L, k2, M1R, pm, knit to end–40 (42) sts. Work even for 2 rnds.
Increase Rnd 4: Knit to first marker, sm, M1L, knit to second marker, M1R, sm, knit to end–42 (44) sts. Work even for 2 rnds.
Repeat last 3 rnds 3 times, then repeat Increase Rnd 4 once–50 (52) sts. Work even for 1 rnd.
Next Rnd: Knit to first marker, transfer next 14 sts to waste yarn, removing Thumb markers, CO 2 sts over gap, knit to end–38 (40) sts remain. Work even in St st until piece is long enough to cover knuckles [approximately 11 (12) rnds].
Next Rnd: Change to 1x1 Rib. Work even for 3 rnds. BO all sts in Rib.

Thumb

Transfer 14 sts from waste yarn to dpns. Rejoin yarn; pick up and knit 2 sts from sts CO over gap–16 sts. Join for working in the rnd; pm for beginning of rnd. Begin 1x1 Rib. Work even for 3 rnds. BO all sts in Rib.

Finishing

Weave in ends. Block Fingerless Gloves.

TAPISSERIE

Worked in the round and edged with Latvian braid, these arm warmers combine motifs inspired by medieval tapestries with a long-established detail of folk-knitting. The result is a sophisticated accessory that can be worn as a casual adornment or for utilitarian warmth. Before central heating, tapestries kept drafts out of cold, stone-walled rooms, and also displayed the wealth of the owner, as they were expensive to commission. With these, you can keep the draft out of your sleeves while displaying your knitting prowess.

braids

SIZES

One size (to fit average woman)

FINISHED MEASUREMENTS

Approximately 7¾" wrist circumference; approximately 10" forearm circumference; approximately 7¼" long

YARN

Reynolds Whiskey (100% wool; 195 yards [177 meters] / 50 grams): 1 ball each #16 burgundy heather (MC) and #103 chartreuse heather (A)

NEEDLES

One set of five double-pointed needles (dpn) size US 3 (3.25 mm)
Change needle size if necessary to obtain correct gauge.

NOTIONS

Stitch markers

GAUGE

28 sts and 30 rnds = 4" (10 cm) in Stockinette stitch (St st) over Fair Isle Chart

STITCH PATTERN

Latvian Braid
(multiple of 2 sts + 1; 3-rnd repeat)
Rnd 1: *K1 with MC, k1 with A; repeat from * to last st, k1 with MC.
Rnd 2: With both yarns at front of work, p1 with MC, *bring A over MC and p1, bring MC over A and p1; repeat from * around. *[Note: Yarns will be twisted after this rnd, but will be untwisted on Rnd 3.]*
Rnd 3: With both yarns at front of work, p1 with MC, *bring A under MC and p1, bring MC under A and p1; repeat from * around.

Arm Warmers (both alike)

With Long-Tail CO (see page 136) and MC, CO 54 sts, divide among 4 needles [14-13-14-13]. Join for working in the rnd, being careful not to twist sts; place marker (pm) for beginning of rnd.
Next Rnd: K7, pm, purl to end.
Next Rnd: [K1 with MC, k1 with A] 3 times, k1 with MC, slip marker (sm), change to Latvian Braid and work to end. Repeat last rnd once.
Next Rnd: [K1 with A, k1 with MC] 3 times, k1 with A, sm, work to end in Latvian Braid.
Next Rnd: Work 7 sts as established, sm, change to MC and knit to end, carrying A behind MC.

BEGIN CHART

Next Rnd: Work 16 sts of Chart, pm, work to last 9 sts of Chart, pm, work to end. Work even for 3 rnds.
Next Rnd (Rnd 5 of Chart): Work to second marker, sm, work to next marker working increases as indicated, sm, work to end–56 sts. Work even until Chart is complete, continuing to work increases between second and third markers, as indicated in Chart–70 sts.
Next Rnd: Work 7 sts as established, change to Latvian Braid and work to end. Repeat last rnd twice. Cut A.
Next Rnd: With MC, knit.
Next Rnd: BO 7 sts knitwise, BO to end purlwise.

FINISHING

Weave in ends. Block Arm Warmers to measurements.

FAIR ISLE CHART

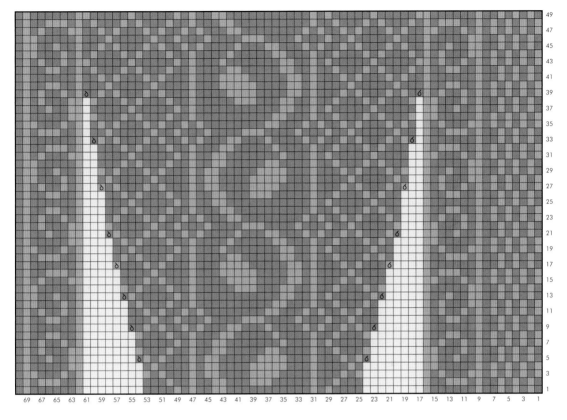

KEY

- ▨ Knit with MC.
- ▨ Knit with A.
- ☐ No stitch
- ◔ M1R
- ◑ M1L

WELIG

The namesake of this pattern is the Old English
name for willow, a water-loving tree known to
occasionally break through concrete with its roots
in search of water. The cables of this glove twist
and climb all the way up the fingers, becoming
entangled with each other on the way, perhaps
seeking water (or snow). Bobbles represent
knotted bark. Some of the cables on these gloves
actually travel through one another, likening
them to the branches of a tree that grow so close
that one begins to grow around the other.

Cables through Cables

SIZES

One size (to fit average woman)

FINISHED MEASUREMENTS

Approximately 7½" circumference

YARN

Nashua Handknits Julia (50% wool / 25% mohair/ 25% alpaca; 93 yards [84 meters] / 50 grams): 2 skeins #4936 blue thyme

NEEDLES

One set of five double-pointed needles (dpn) size US 6 (4 mm)
Change needle size if necessary to obtain correct gauge.

NOTIONS

Stitch markers; 2 cable needles (cn); waste yarn in contrasting color; tapestry needle

GAUGE

21 sts and 29 rnds = 4" (10 cm) in Stockinette stitch (St st)
26 sts = 3¾" (9.5 cm) over Cable Chart, after Rnd 23

NOTE

You will have to rearrange the sts between Needles 1 and 2 occasionally in order to complete certain cables and bobbles. Reposition them once you have finished the necessary maneuver.

ABBREVIATIONS

RT (Right Twist): Knit into front of second st, then knit into front of first st, slip both sts from left-hand needle together.

LT (Left Twist): Knit into back of second st, then knit into front of first st, slip both sts from left-hand needle together.

Right Glove

Using Long-Tail CO (see page 136), CO 42 sts, divide among 4 needles [12-12-9-9]. Join for working in the rnd, being careful not to twist sts; place marker (pm) for beginning of rnd. *[Note: Needles 1 and 2 hold the sts for the back of the hand, and Needles 3 and 4 hold the sts for the palm.]*

Rnd 1: Work Cable Chart across 24 sts, pm, *k2, p2; repeat from * to last 2 sts, k2. Work even until Rnd 23 of Chart has been completed.

Increase Rnd: Working increases as indicated in Chart, work across Chart to first marker, sm, k1, M1R, knit to last st, M1L, k1–46 sts. Work even, working from Chart to first marker, and in St st to end, until Rnd 39 of Chart has been completed.

THUMB OPENING

Next Rnd: Work to first marker, k1, change to waste yarn and k7, slip these 7 sts back to left-hand needle, change to working yarn, knit these 7 sts again, work to end. Work even until Rnd 50 of Chart has been completed.

Decrease Rnd (Rnd 51): P2tog, k1, LT, p1, p2tog, k3, [p2tog] twice, k3, p1, p2tog, k1, LT, p2, knit to end, removing markers–41 sts remain.

DIVIDE FOR FINGERS

Transfer all sts from Needle 2 to Needle 1 for back of hand, and all sts from Needle 4 to Needle 3 for palm. *[Note: Use a piece of waste yarn threaded on a tapestry needle to hold the sts for each finger.]*

Pinkie: Transfer first 5 sts from Needle 1 and last 5 sts from Needle 3 to waste yarn–10 sts. **Ring Finger:** Transfer next 5 sts from Needle 1 and next 4 sts from Needle 3 to waste yarn–9 sts. **Middle Finger:** Transfer next 5 sts from each of Needles 1 and 3 to waste yarn–10 sts. **Index Finger:** Transfer remaining 6 sts from each of Needles 1 and 3 to waste yarn–12 sts.

PINKIE

Transfer sts from waste yarn to dpns.

Set-Up Rnd: P1, k3, p1, CO 2 sts over gap between Pinkie and Ring Finger, k5–12 sts. Join for working in the rnd; pm for beginning of rnd.

Rnd 1: P1, RT, k1, p1, knit to end.

Rnds 2 and 4: P1, k3, p1, knit to end.

Rnd 3: P1, k1, LT, p1, knit to end.

Repeat Rnds 1–4 until piece is long enough to cover Pinkie (approximately 16 rnds).

Decrease Rnd: *K2tog; repeat from * around–6 sts remain. Cut yarn, leaving a 6" tail. Draw through remaining sts, pull tight and fasten off to the inside.

Ring Finger and Middle Finger

Working one Finger at a time, transfer sts from waste yarn to dpns. Rejoin yarn; pick up and knit 2 sts from sts CO for previous Finger, p1, k3, p1, CO 2 sts over gap between current Finger and next Finger, knit to end–13 sts for Ring Finger; 14 sts for Middle Finger. Join for working in the rnd; pm for beginning of rnd.

Rnd 1: K2, p1, k3, p1, knit to end. Repeat Rnd 1 until piece is long enough to cover finger (approximately 20 rnds for Ring Finger; 22 rnds for Middle Finger).

Decrease Rnd: [K2tog] 6 times (7 times for Middle Finger), k1 (0 for Middle Finger)–7 sts remain. Complete as for Pinkie.

Index Finger

Transfer sts from waste yarn to dpns. Rejoin yarn; pick up and knit 2 sts from sts CO for Middle Finger, p1, k3, p2, k6–14 sts. Join for working in the rnd; pm for beginning of rnd.

Rnd 1: K2, p1, RT, k1, p2, knit to end.

Rnds 2 and 4: K2, p1, k3, p2, knit to end.

Rnd 3: K2, p1, k1, LT, p2, knit to end.

Repeat Rnds 1-4 until piece is long enough to cover Index Finger (approximately 21 rnds). Complete as for Pinkie–7 sts remain.

Thumb

Carefully remove waste yarn from Thumb sts and place bottom 7 sts and top 8 sts onto dpns, being careful not to twist sts. Rejoin yarn to bottom sts, pick up and knit 2 sts at side of Thumb Opening, knit across 7 bottom sts, pick up and knit 2 sts at other side of Thumb Opening, knit across 8 top sts–19 sts. Redistribute sts among 3 dpns. Join for working in the rnd; pm for beginning of rnd.

Next Rnd: K1, k2tog, k5, ssk, k2tog, k6, ssk (last st of rnd together with first st of next rnd)–15 sts remain. Work even in St st until piece is long enough to cover Thumb (approximately 20 rnds).

Decrease Rnd: [K2tog] 7 times, k1–8 sts remain. Complete as for Pinkie.

Left Glove

Work as for Right Glove to Thumb Opening.

Thumb Opening

Next Rnd: Work to first marker, k12, change to waste yarn and k7, slip these 7 sts back to left-hand needle, change to working yarn, knit these 7 sts again, k1. Work even until Rnd 50 of Chart has been completed.

Decrease Rnd (Rnd 51): P2, k1, LT, p2tog, p1, k3, [p2tog] twice, k3, p2tog, p1, k1, LT, p2tog, knit to end, removing markers–41 sts remain.

Divide for Fingers

Transfer sts for fingers to waste yarn as for Right Glove, reversing the order in which the fingers lie (begin with the Index Finger and end with the Pinkie).

Index Finger

Transfer sts from waste yarn to dpns.

Set-up Rnd: P2, k3, p1, CO 2 sts over gap between Index Finger and Middle Finger, k6–14 sts. Join for working in the rnd; pm for beginning of rnd.

Rnd 1: P2, RT, k1, p1, knit to end.

Rnds 2 and 4: P2, k3, p1, knit to end.

Rnd 3: P2, k1, LT, p1, knit to end.

Complete as for Right Index Finger.

Middle Finger and Ring Finger

Work as for Right Glove, reversing order.

Pinkie

Transfer sts from waste yarn to dpns.

Set-up Rnd: Pick up and knit 2 sts from sts CO for Ring Finger, p1, k3, p1, k5–12 sts. Join for working in the rnd; pm for beginning of rnd.

Rnd 1: K2, p1, RT, k1, p1, knit to end.

Rnds 2 and 4: K2, p1, k3, p1, knit to end.

Rnd 3: K2, p1, k1, LT, p1, knit to end.

Complete as for Right Pinkie.

Complete as for Right Glove.

CABLE CHART

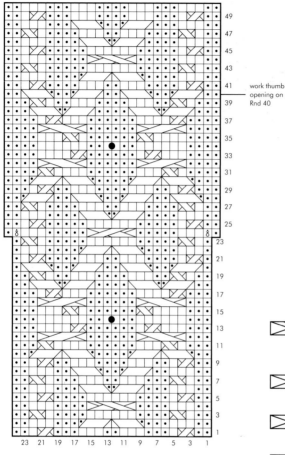

work thumb
opening on
Rnd 40

KEY

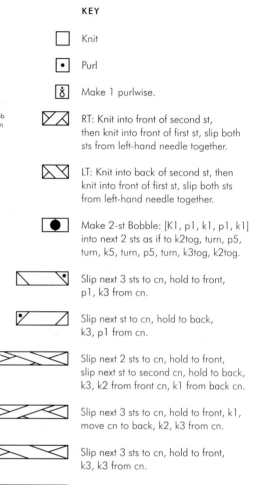

☐ Knit

• Purl

Make 1 purlwise.

RT: Knit into front of second st, then knit into front of first st, slip both sts from left-hand needle together.

LT: Knit into back of second st, then knit into front of first st, slip both sts from left-hand needle together.

Make 2-st Bobble: [K1, p1, k1, p1, k1] into next 2 sts as if to k2tog, turn, p5, turn, k5, turn, p5, turn, k3tog, k2tog.

Slip next 3 sts to cn, hold to front, p1, k3 from cn.

Slip next st to cn, hold to back, k3, p1 from cn.

Slip next 2 sts to cn, hold to front, slip next st to second cn, hold to back, k3, k2 from front cn, k1 from back cn.

Slip next 3 sts to cn, hold to front, k1, move cn to back, k2, k3 from cn.

Slip next 3 sts to cn, hold to front, k3, k3 from cn.

Slip next 3 sts to cn, hold to back, k3, k3 from cn.

YARN

I like to knit with yarns made from natural fibers because they are so beautiful and feel the best in my hands. When choosing the yarns for the mittens and gloves in this book, I kept in mind the amount and type of wear they were likely to sustain. If you are planning to substitute yarns, I suggest you consider the same. I think Icelandic wool, Shetland wool, and mohair are all excellent choices for winter mittens and gloves that will be worn a lot because they are warm and strong and don't pill a lot. I also like alpaca, which is silky and four times warmer than wool, for luxurious items. There are many patterns in this book that are intended for multi-seasonal and indoor wear; for these, I suggest cottons, soft wools, fine silk, and cashmere blends.

NEEDLES

Most of the patterns in this book are knit in the round on double-pointed needles. I prefer sets of five over sets of four, as the mittens and the hand part of gloves can be divided on four needles such that the stitches for front and back are each on two needles. This makes it easier for working shaping, and for generally visualizing the finished product. A set of five needles also has the advantage that if you lose or break one, you will be able to manage with the remaining four. Any pattern can certainly be knit with a set of four needles if you prefer. Many people enjoy knitting in the round using the magic loop technique and one long circular needle; see the bibliography for information on the book that popularized this technique.

For mittens and gloves, it is best to use double-pointed needles that are five to seven inches long. Sometimes they are available longer, but it is cumbersome to use them for small items because the ends of the needles get in the way and the yarn gets tangled around them. If you make a lot of gloves, consider investing in some glove needles, which are quite short (about four inches long) and easier to manipulate than longer needles when working the fingers.

Whenever straight needles are called for, I always use a circular needle and work back and forth on it. If you knit a lot or for long hours at a time, or if you suffer from arthritis, doing this will greatly reduce the stress on your wrists and elbows.

When choosing needles, I like to select the metric (millimeter) size rather than the US size. The size in millimeters is an actual measurement, and I find that it is more reliable than the US sizes, which sometimes vary slightly among manufacturers. For example, a US size 6 needle is sometimes 4 mm and sometimes 4.25 mm. A needle gauge is a good tool to have on hand for double-checking.

NOTIONS

Notions are an easy way to customize a plain item. You can sew beads onto the back of a glove, add leather ties, switch leather for ribbon, or embroider with sequins. If you tire of these adornments, they are usually easily changed or snipped off. For ideas, look through fashion magazines, watch people on the street, and notice how clothing designers use notions in ways you have not seen before. I also encourage you to look around in sewing, ribbon, bead, and button shops and to purchase items that appeal to you even if you don't have a specific use in mind. As you live with them you will surely be inspired.

Beading

When you wish to knit with beads, begin by
threading the beads onto the yarn as follows:
Thread the yarn through a wire beading needle,
then thread the beads onto the yarn using the
beading needle. Push the beads down the yarn
so there is enough yarn with which to cast on
and begin knitting. In the Evening Light pattern
(see page 55), the beads are placed from the wrong
side so that they fall to the right side. Working in
Garter stitch on the wrong side, slide
a bead up close to the needle and knit the next
stitch. Note that the bead is actually sitting
between two stitches on the horizontal strand.
In the Box Pleats pattern (see page 29), the beads
are placed from the right side of the work in two
ways: 1) they are placed between two purl stitches
on the horizontal strand (just like how they are
placed when working in Garter stitch) by purling
the first stitch, pushing the bead up close to the
needle and purling the next stitch; and 2), they are
placed on a yarn float sitting in front of a slipped
stitch, by slipping the next stitch purlwise with
the yarn in front, pushing the bead up close to
the needle, then working the next stitch as
directed. Use a pair of needle-nose pliers to crush
off any small or misshapen beads that you may
have inadvertently strung. Be careful not to
inadvertently cut the yarn when crushing the
beads. Crush them into your hand and dispose
of them safely.

Blocking

Although mittens and gloves generally do not
need to be blocked to a specific shape or set
of measurements, it is a good idea to block them
to even out any irregularities in your stitches.
This is especially important if you will be picking
up stitches, or working duplicate stitch or
embroidery. It also finishes the fabric nicely,
giving your work a professional look.

I usually block mittens and gloves with a steam
iron and damp cloth. Place the item on the ironing
board. Pin out anything that you want to take
on a specific shape (ruffles, etc). Place the damp
cloth (a white cotton tea towel dampened with
cold water is a perfect press-cloth) on top of the
item. Take the iron, preheated to the wool setting,
and run it lightly over the cloth while pressing
the steam burst button. Don't press the iron down
hard or linger over one spot. If you are blocking
cables—which you would not want to flatten—
hold the iron above the cloth while you steam it.
If the item is made of a fragile material, like silk
or viscose, use a double thickness of damp cloth,
hold the iron above the cloth, and fire short
bursts of steam. It does not take a lot of heat and
moisture to set fabrics such as these. Never place
the iron directly on the knitting. If the press-cloth
begins to dry, wet it again. If your stitches are
very uneven or if you are blocking lace, you are
likely to get better results by immersing the item
in a basin of lukewarm water, then rolling it in
a towel to squeeze out the excess moisture, and
pinning it out to dry flat.

Casting On

BACKWARD LOOP CO

This is the easiest and least obtrusive way to cast on stitches over a thumb hole, especially if you will be picking up from them later. *Wind the yarn around your thumb clockwise, insert right-hand needle into the front of the loop on the thumb, remove the thumb and tighten the stitch on the needle; repeat from * for remaining sts to be CO, or for casting on at the end of a row in progress.

LONG-TAIL CO (GERMAN METHOD)

This is the method I use most often. It is elastic, attractive, versatile and easy to work. Leaving a tail with about 1" of yarn for each st to be cast-on, make a slipknot in the yarn and place it on the right-hand needle, with the tail to the front and the ball end to the back. *Note: I usually leave the tail extra-long and use the excess to sew with.* Insert the thumb and forefinger of your left hand between the strands of yarn so that the working end is around your forefinger, and the tail end is around your thumb "slingshot" fashion; *insert the tip of the right-hand needle into the front loop on the thumb, hook the strand of yarn coming from the forefinger from back to front, and draw it through the loop on your thumb; remove your thumb from the loop and pull on the working yarn to tighten the new stitch on the right-hand needle; return your thumb and forefinger to their original positions, and repeat from * for the remaining stitches to be CO.

Embroidery

CLOSED BLANKET STITCH

This stitch is worked around an edge (as shown in the illustration below). Thread the tapestry needle with no more than an arm's length of yarn. Hold the end of the yarn parallel to the edge of the knitting. Bring the needle through from the right side to the wrong side about ¼" from the top edge, bringing it in front of the yarn at the top edge so that it forms a "corner." *Bring needle tip from the right side to the wrong side again, ¼" from the edge, holding the needle tip in front of the yarn at the top edge. Repeat from *, making stitches very close together, and pulling yarn tightly. Note that this is the same as Blanket Stitch, except that the stitches are closer together.

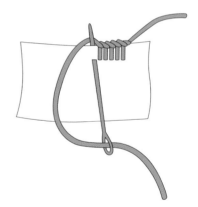

French Knots

Thread the tapestry needle with no more than an arm's length of yarn. Bring the needle up from the wrong side at the spot where you wish to make the knot. *Note: You may bring the needle up through the middle of a strand of yarn, rather than next to one, as this will help your knot sit on the surface.* With the needle lying next to where the yarn comes out, wrap the embroidery yarn 2 or 3 times tightly around the needle tip (as shown in the illustration below). Hold the wrapped yarn in place with your finger as you bring the needle to the wrong side again about ⅛" from where it came up last, pulling the rest of the working yarn through the knot. The knot sits on the surface.

Duplicate Stitch

Thread the tapestry needle with no more than an arm's length of yarn. Bring the needle up from the wrong side at the base of a stitch (the pointed end of the "v"). *Thread the yarn under both ends of the stitch above the one you wish to duplicate, following the line that the yarn of the existing stitch takes. Bring the needle back to the wrong side at the base of the stitch again, then to the right side at the base of the next stitch to be duplicated. Repeat from *. You can work from left to right or right to left. Since in most cases you will not be seeing the wrong side of the work, you can bring the needle up again short distances from the last stitch duplicated if you need to work into another row. Note that you have covered the original stitches with the new color.

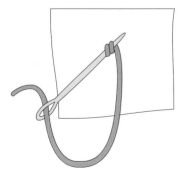

I-Cord

STANDARD I-CORD

Using a double-pointed needle, cast on the required number of stitches (3 or 4); the working yarn will be at the left-hand side of the needle. *Transfer the needle with the stitches to your left hand, bring the yarn around behind the work to the right-hand side; using a second double-pointed needle, knit the stitches from right to left, pulling the yarn from left to right for the first stitch; do not turn. Slide the stitches to the opposite end of the needle; repeat from * until the I-cord is the length desired. *Note: After a few rows, the tubular shape will become apparent.* Cut the yarn, leaving a 6" tail. Draw through the remaining stitches, pull tight and fasten off.

APPLIED I-CORD

Using a double-pointed needle, cast on the required number of stitches (3 or 4); the working yarn will be at the left-hand side of the needle. *With the wrong side of the edge to which you will apply the I-cord facing you, pick up and knit 1 st. Working as for I-cord, slide the stitches to the opposite end of the needle, pulling the yarn from left to right for the first stitch, knit to the last 2 sts, k2tog-tbl. Repeat from * to the end of the edge to which the I-cord is to be applied. *Note: If the I-cord is worked with the WS facing, the end result on the RS is smoother and neater than if the stitches were picked with the RS facing. Notice that the decrease will appear on the WS of the work.* Cut the yarn, leaving a 6" tail. Draw through the remaining stitches, pull tight and fasten off.

I-CORD BO

Using a double-pointed needle, cast on the required number of stitches; the working yarn will be at the left-hand side of the needle. *With the wrong side of the edge to be bound off facing you, slip the first stitch to be bound off knitwise onto the left-hand end of the I-cord needle. Working as for I-cord, slide the stitches to the opposite end of the needle, pulling the yarn from left to right for the first stitch, knit to the last 2 sts, k2tog-tbl. Repeat from * until all stitches are bound off. *Note: If the I-cord is worked with the WS facing, the end result on the RS is smoother and neater than if the stitches were picked with the RS facing. Notice that the decrease will appear on the WS of the work.* Cut the yarn, leaving a 6" tail. Draw through the remaining stitches, pull tight and fasten off.

Kitchener Stitch

Using a tapestry needle, thread length of yarn approximately 4 times the length of section to be joined. Hold pieces to be joined with WS's together, with needles holding sts parallel, both ends pointing in same direction. Working from right to left, insert tapestry needle into first st on front needle as if to purl, pull yarn through, leaving st on needle; insert tapestry needle into first st on back needle as if to knit, pull yarn through, leaving st on needle; *insert tapestry needle into first st on front needle as if to knit, pull yarn through, removing st from needle; insert tapestry needle into next st on front needle as if to purl, pull yarn through, leaving st on needle; insert tapestry needle into first st on back needle as if to purl, pull yarn through, removing st from needle; insert tapestry needle into next st on back needle as if to knit, pull yarn through, leaving st on needle. Repeat from *, working 3 or 4 sts at a time, then go back and adjust tension to match pieces being joined. When 1 st remains on each needle, cut yarn and pass through last 2 sts to fasten off. Weave tail in on WS. Note that you are sewing through two sts at a time, back and forth between front and back needles, and that every st will be worked into twice (once through each side of st).

Reading Charts

Unless otherwise specified in the instructions, when working straight, charts are read from right to left for RS rows, and from left to right for WS rows. Row numbers are written at the beginning of each row. Numbers on the right indicate RS rows; numbers on the left indicate WS rows. When working circular, all rounds are read from right to left.

Short Row Shaping

Short row shaping is used to shape the knitting by working some, but not all, of the stitches on a given row. This creates a wedge shape of varying width and depth, depending on the number of stitches worked and the number of short rows worked. Work the number of stitches specified in the pattern, then wrap and turn (wrp-t) as follows: bring the yarn to the front, slip the next stitch purlwise, bring the yarn to the back, slip the same stitch back to the left-hand needle, and turn the work. Work back to the end of the row (or as indicated in the pattern). Wrapping the stitch prevents a hole from forming where you turned the work. Where it specifies in the directions to knit or purl a wrapped stitch together with its wrap, do exactly that. Lift the wrap up onto the needle (this makes it easier to work) and knit or purl it together with the next stitch. This hides the wrap so that it isn't visible on the right side. You do not need to hide the wrap in Garter stitch, because the nature of the pattern hides it for you.

Stranded (Fair Isle) Colorwork Method

This method is used when working with more than one color per row, in which both colors are carried along the whole row. I usually hold one color in each hand when working with two colors. You can hold one color on each of two fingers of one hand if you prefer. Hold the dominant yarn (this is the pattern color, the one you want to stand out more) in the position where it will always be carried underneath the background color—in the left hand if you are carrying the colors in two hands. These stitches will be slightly larger than the background stitches. If you need to carry one color more than 3 or 4 stitches along, twist it in with the other color along the wrong side so that the float is not too long. Otherwise, float the yarn not in use along the wrong side of the work. Every few stitches, pull the stitches just worked apart from each other a bit—this prevents your work from getting too tight. If you are combining colorwork with plain knitting in the same project, it is a good idea to use a needle one size larger for the colorwork than for the plain knitting, as most knitters will knit more tightly in stranded colorwork.

BO – Bind off.

Ch – Chain.

CO – Cast on.

Dcd (double centered decrease) – Slip next 2 sts together knitwise to right-hand needle, k1, pass 2 slipped sts over knit stitch.

Dpn – Double-pointed needle(s).

K – Knit.

K2tog – Knit 2 sts together.

K2tog-tbl – Knit 2 sts together through back loops.

K3tog – Knit 3 sts together.

K1-f/b – Knit into front loop and back loop of same stitch to increase one stitch.

K1-tbl – Knit one stitch through the back loop, twisting the stitch.

MB – Make bobble (as instructed).

M1R (make 1-right slanting) – With the tip of the left-hand needle inserted from back to front, lift the strand between the two needles onto the left-hand needle; knit it through the front loop to increase one stitch.

M1 or M1L (make 1-left slanting) – With the tip of the left-hand needle inserted from front to back, lift the strand between the two needles onto the left-hand needle; knit the strand through the back loop to increase one stitch.

M1P (make 1 purlwise) - With the tip of the left-hand needle inserted from back to front, lift the strand between the two needles onto the left-hand needle; purl the strand through the front loop to increase one stitch.

P – Purl.

P2tog – Purl 2 sts together.

P1-f/b – Purl the next st through the front of its loop, then through the back of its loop, to increase one st.

Pm – Place marker.

Psso (pass slipped stitch over) – Pass slipped st on right-hand needle over the sts indicated in the instructions, as in binding off.

Rnd(s) – Round(s).

RS – Right side.

Sk2p (double decrease) – Slip next st knitwise to right-hand needle, k2tog, pass slipped st over st from k2tog.

Sm – Slip marker.

Ssk (slip, slip, knit) – Slip the next 2 sts to the right-hand needle one at a time as if to knit; return them back to left-hand needle one at a time in their new orientation; knit them together through the back loop(s).

Ssp (slip, slip, purl) – Slip the next 2 sts to right-hand needle one at a time as if to knit; return them to the left-hand needle one at a time in their new orientation; purl them together through the back loop(s).

St(s) – Stitch(es).

Tbl – Through the back loop.

WS – Wrong side.

Wrp-t – Wrap and turn (see Special Techniques, Short Row Shaping).

Wyib – With yarn in back.

Wyif – With yarn in front.

Yo (Yarnover) – Bring the yarn forward (to the purl position), then place it in position to work the next stitch. If the next stitch is to be knit, bring the yarn over the needle and knit; if the next stitch is to be purled, bring the yarn over the needle and then forward again to the purl position and purl. Work the yarnover in pattern on the next row unless instructed otherwise.

Refer to this list when choosing yarn for the projects. Sometimes a fancy stitch pattern will produce a different gauge than would be marked on the yarn's label, which is always over Stockinette stitch. Also, mittens and gloves are generally knit a bit tighter than a sweater would be (yarn label gauges are for an average sweater fabric). This list will prevent you from being misled by these differences.

Fingering (30-34 sts/4")
Blackthorn (also uses Double Knitting yarn), page 25
Golden Bracelets, page 69

4-ply (27-29 sts/4")
Rusalka, page 103
Standard Deviation, page 115

Sport (24-26 sts/4")
Evening Light, page 55
Glaistig, page 65
Poppy (also uses Double Knitting yarn), page 99
Strata, page 119
Tapisserie, page 125

Double Knitting (DK) (22-23 sts/4")
Ålesund, page 17
Blackthorn (also uses Fingering yarn), page 25
Box Pleats, page 29
Ceangaltas, page 41
Driver, page 49
Poppy (also uses Sport yarn), page 99

Worsted (19-21 sts/4")
Brünnhilde, page 35
Filigree, page 61
Houndstooth Miscellany, page 81
Jack-in-the-Box, page 85
Strata, page 119
Welig, page 129

Aran (17-18 sts/4")
Accomplice, page 9
Aethelwyne, page 13
Gothic, page 73
Gretel (also uses Bulky yarn), page 77
Sheltie (also uses Bulky yarn), page 107
Snug, page 111

Chunky (15-16 sts/4")
Plush, page 95

Bulky (12-14 sts/4")
Alternating Current, page 21
Gretel (also uses Aran yarn), page 77
Negative Space, page 91
Sheltie (also uses Aran yarn), page 107

Super Bulky (9-11 sts/4")
Chevalier, page 45

Blue Sky Alpacas
PO Box 88
Cedar, MN 55011
1-888-460-8862
www.blueskyalpacas.com

Brown Sheep Company
100662 County Road 16
Mitchell, NE 69357
1-800-826-9136
www.brownsheep.com

Estelle Designs
Canadian distributor
of Dale of Norway,
Jo Sharp Yarns
2220 Midland Avenue,
Unit 65
Scarborough, ON
M1P 3E6 Canada
1-416-298-9922
www.estelleyarns.com

**Fleece Artist/Hand
Maiden**
www.fleeceartist.com
www.handmaiden.ca

Garnstudio
Dist. in Canada by
Nordic Yarn Imports Ltd.
#301-5327 192nd Street
Surrey, BC
V3S 8E5 Canada
1-604-574-4445 ·
www.garnstudio.com

Dist. in USA by
Aurora Yarns
PO Box 3068
Moss Beach, CA 94038
1-650-728-2730
www.garnstudio.com

Harrisville Designs
Center Village,
PO Box 806
Harrisville, NH 03450
1-800-338-9415
www.harrisville.com

JCA, Inc./Reynolds
35 Scales Lane
Townsend, MA
01469-1094
1-978-597-8794
www.jcacrafts.com

Manos del Uruguay
Dist. in Canada by
Ashley Yarns
334 Ottawa St. North
Hamilton, ON
L8H 4A1 Canada
1-866-919-0995
www.ashleyyarns.com

Dist. in USA by
Fairmount Fibers
915 N. 28th St.
Philadelphia, PA 19130
1-888-566-9970
www.fairmountfibers.com

Mountain Colors
PO Box 156
Corvallis, MT 59828
1-406-961-1900
www.mountaincolors.com

Nashua Handknits
Dist. by Westminster Fibers
165 Ledge St.
Nashua, NH 03060
1-800-445-9276
www.westminsterfibers.com

Nordic Fiber Arts
4 Cutts Road
Durham, NH 03824
1-603-868-1196
www.nordicfiberarts.com

Oberlyn Yarns
Canadian distributor
of Inca Gold Collection
and Muench yarns
and buttons
5640 Rue Valcourt
Brossard, QC
J4W 1C5 Canada
1-450-672-0777
www.oberlyn.ca

Naturally Yarns
Dist. in Canada by
The Old Mill Knitting
Company
F.G. PO Box 81176
Ancaster, ON
L9G 4X2 Canada
1-866-964-9941
www.oldmillknitting.com

Dist. in USA by Fiber Trends
PO Box 7266
East Wenatchee, WA
98802-7266
1-509-884-8631
www.fibertrends.com

Rowan
Dist. by Westminster Fibers
165 Ledge St.
Nashua, NH 03060
1-800-445-9276
www.westminsterfibers.com

Simply Shetland
10 Domingo Road
Santa Fe, NM 87508
1-505-466-3044
www.simplyshetland.net

**Tandy Leather
Factory, Inc.**
(leather and suede lacing)
3847 East Loop 820 South
Fort Worth, TX 76119
1-800-433-3201
www.tandyleatherfactory.com

BIBLIOGRAPHY

Brown-Reinsel, Beth. *Knitting Ganseys.* Loveland, Colorado: Interweave Press, 1993.

---. "Beyond the Basics: Working with Two Yarns." *Interweave Knits.* Summer 2004, Volume IX, Number 2, pp. 68-72.

Fossnes, Heidi. *Håndplagg til bunader og folkedrakter.* Oslo, Norway: N. W. Damm & Søn AS, 2004.

Galeskas, Bev and Hauschka, Sarah. *The Magic Loop.* East Wenatchee, WA: Fiber Trends, 2002. Booklet distributed by Fiber Trends (USA) and The Old Mill Knitting Company (Canada).

Upitis, Lizbeth. *Latvian Mittens.* Pittsville, Wisconsin: Schoolhouse Press, 1997.

Walker, Barbara G. *A Treasury of Knitting Patterns.* Pittsville, Wisconsin: Schoolhouse Press, 1998.

ACKNOWLEDGEMENTS

A very special thank you to my partner Craig, who graciously agrees that it does indeed take a rather large mountain of yarn to produce 28+ pairs of mittens and gloves; and to Julia Grunau for her moral support during the looming of deadlines.

Thank you to Sue McCain for helping the patterns attain a level of perfection that would make the Borg envious; to photographer Tyllie Barbosa and stylist Kelly McKaig for their beautiful images and their wondrous collection of props; to graphic designer Sarah Von Dreele for her ability to combine everyone's efforts so seamlessly and logically; to JC Briar for her 'extra eyes'; to Liana Allday for her great job with the onerous task of reviewing the text (and deciphering my handwritten comments); and a big giant thank you to editor Melanie Falick for believing in me and for saying out loud what I'm thinking in my head.

Thank you also to all the companies who were so generous in their yarn support: your wonderful products bring me joy. Special thanks to all the knitters with cold hands: I hope you enjoy making and wearing the things in this book as much as I enjoyed working on them.